1951

THE STORY OF THE U. S. MARINES

THE STORY
OF THE
U.S. MARINES

★

by GEORGE P. HUNT

Illustrated by CHARLES J. MAZOUJIAN

RANDOM HOUSE · NEW YORK

CONTENTS

THE STORY OF THE U. S. MARINES

Korea: November, 1950

1

FIRST LIEUTENANT JOHN YANCEY of the United States Marines raised his binoculars to his eyes and studied the land in front of him. A valley ran to the north. At the bottom of it a dirt road passed through a cluster of shacks called Sudong and curled like a white ribbon into the icy mountain passes miles ahead. Along the valley slopes, wherever Yancey could see, scrubby ridges writhed in every direction.

3

This was North Korea—a bleak and almost treeless land. It was frigid cold—at night the temperature would drop to thirty degrees below zero—and it was filled with danger. The ridges and slopes, which seemed to look more threatening each day, were infested with a tenacious enemy—tens of thousands of Chinese Communist soldiers.

For a long time Lieutenant Yancey kept his binoculars fixed on one jagged ridge 250 yards away. On his map this ridge was a scraggle of fine, wavy lines marked Hill 698. Actually, it was a natural fortress defended by a Chinese battalion armed with rifles, machine guns, hand-grenades, and big mortars. On top of it a mass of solid rock rose up like the remains of an old chimney, while its sides fell off in steep and at some places perpendicular slopes.

Yancey swore to himself softly. There was only one route by which this stronghold could be attacked. That was along a finger of scrub-covered ground that led to it from the knoll on which he was lying. But this route was so narrow that barely more than thirty men could make the assault at one time, while the defending Chinese could mass more than a hundred.

Again and again Hill 698 had beaten off attack.

South Korean troops had assaulted it and failed, and Yancey could see their dead piled in heaps. Company D of the 7th Marine Regiment, First Marine Division, had stormed it twice without success. Then E Company had been brought into position and it had sent its 3rd platoon attacking along the narrow finger. The platoon had reached the foot of the ridge, then halfway up. Barrages of Chinese hand-grenades had poured on top of the oncoming men and machine guns had swept them from the sides. Not many marines had come back.

Hill 698 was a key position in the line of Chinese defenses scattered through the ridges and it had to be taken. Now—it was 3:00 P.M., November 4th, 1950—the job of taking it had fallen to the 2nd platoon of Company E, thirty-two men strong, commanded by Lieutenant Yancey.

Yancey pulled out a notebook and a stubby pencil from his breast pocket and made a sketch of Hill 698, putting on it the details he had noted through his binoculars. Pointing to his sketch, he gave his orders for the attack to his NCO's. Sergeant Cagolitti—a quiet man, with ink-black hair—would take his squad along the right side of the scrub-covered finger; Corporal Phillips—blond, mild-looking—

would attack on the left. Platoon Sergeant Madding —a hard-bitten veteran of many fights—would go with Phillips' squad; Yancey himself would place himself on the right with Cagolitti.

"When we get halfway up the ridge," said Yancey, remembering what had happened to the third platoon, "throw two barrages of hand-grenades. Then charge before the Chinese can do the same to us."

Soon after Yancey had given his orders, four Corsairs came in to work over Hill 698. They zoomed low, but their rockets missed the hill, and the napalm bomb, dropping fifty yards away from it, burst into oily flames that burned harmlessly. At the same time the Chinese, sensing that an attack was coming, began peppering E Company's position with machine guns. The bullets snapped viciously overhead.

Yancey jumped to his field telephone and talked to Lieutenant Ball, the executive officer of Company E.

"Ray, the planes haven't hit anything. Can you call in another strike?"

"No, sorry," came Ball's crisp reply. "Time is running out. We have to take that hill before dark."

Time *was* running out. Daylight was beginning to fade and shadows were darkening the valley. So, with the precision that comes with years of experience, Yancey got himself ready for the battle. He rolled out of his hooded coat. He clamped a bayonet on the end of his carbine which he cocked. He pulled back the slide of his 45-caliber automatic so that it too was ready to be fired. He stuffed handgrenades into his pockets and hung them on his pistol belt. Then he signaled the gunners of his machine guns to start spraying Hill 698.

Above the snapping of the enemy bullets, above the raving of his own machine guns, Lieutenant Yancey bellowed out his commands. "Fix bayonets! Take the hill, Cagolitti! Take it, Phillips!"

Off they went, that platoon of thirty-two men, in the savage rhythm of the assault, running, falling, shooting, getting up, and running again. The earth on the finger of land shook as Chinese mortars pounded across it, scattering fragments of steel. The shell bursts struck close to Hill 698 at first, then crept down the finger toward the advancing marines. To be caught in it would mean certain destruction. Phillips' squad held up for an instant. But through the mortar blasts they heard Lieutenant Yancey's shout: "Run through it! Run through it!"

This they did in a charge that carried them half-way up the face of Hill 698. But on the right the advance had left a trail of gray-green. Cagolitti had been shot, and a tousle-headed private named Robinson had taken command of the squad. He drove it on up the steep, rocky slope to a position even with Phillips. Down came the Chinese hand-grenades, striking full in the middle of the marines, but back went a barrage of marine grenades followed by another one fifteen yards farther up the hill. The marines rose and, firing their rifles from their hips, went over the top of 698.

On the flat they ran into the Chinese charging from the other side of the ridge. Private Hultman, carrying a Browning Automatic Rifle, was shot through the groin. He slumped over. Yancey took up Hultman's BAR and set about using it on the Chinese.

In World War II Yancey had been a BAR man with the Marine Raiders and had learned to fire this devastating weapon from the hip. Pivoting on his knee, he swept it back and forth, spraying the enemy soldiers as they came on. In one burst he riddled

six of them. The Chinese shot back with their rapid-
fire "burp" guns. Two bullets went through Yancey's helmet, others ripped into his clothes, but his
body was not scratched. All the while, Hultman,
bleeding at the stomach, crawled around the ridge
gathering BAR ammunition from the dead and
wounded, bringing it back to the Lieutenant.

On the left only Corporal Phillips and three men
survived the charge to the top of the ridge. They did
not stop there, but went on toward the mass of rock
that looked like the ruins of a chimney. Halfway
up it, Phillips saw a Chinese rise from behind a
boulder. A grenade struck him in the stomach and
exploded, but not before he had emptied his "burp"
gun into the face of one of the marines. Phillips
and his last two men gained the summit, and from
there rained grenades and bullets on the Chinese
who remained below.

Out of Sergeant Cagolitti's squad, only Private
Robinson got to the top of the ridge unhurt. There
he stood bolt upright in the face of the Chinese,
hurling grenade after grenade at them. Chinese grenades would strike next to him. Smoke and fragments would engulf him, clear away, and there
Robinson still stood, miraculously unhurt. One of

his grenades landed squarely on a Chinese machine-gun emplacement, throwing up a burst of sparkling white phosphorous that set fire to the crew.

After five more furious minutes, the fight along the ridge began to slacken. With their machine gun gone, the Chinese had decided to pull back. Lieutenant Yancey noticed that his BAR was white hot and that his right hand was burned to his wrist and already blistering.

But though the enemy had withdrawn, the ridge was by no means won. Only six marines were left and the ridge had to be held against the counter-attacks that would certainly come.

Yancey picked up his walkie-talkie radio.

"Hello, Ray," he said to Lieutenant Ball.

"Good work, Yancey. How are you fixed?" came the answer.

"I've got only six men left—have to have more men quick!"

"The first platoon is trying to get through to you," said Lieutenant Ball, "but the Chinese are laying down heavy fire between us from other positions on the right."

Yancey looked back. Mortar shells were indeed pounding the finger of land behind him, and ma-

chine-gun bullets were clipping through the scrub
on top of it. The enemy's plan was simple, he
thought. While they kept him cut off from reinforcements, they would attack him with bayonets
and grenades.

Soon enough, from out of the ravine on the far
side of Hill 698, came the quick piercing notes
of a bugle. The Chinese counterattack was forming.

The 2nd platoon was as ready as it could be—a
thin semi-circle of men with most of their ammunition gone. Yancey had another BAR. Hultman was
alive, but too weak to move. Robinson had three
grenades left. Phillips was still crouched on top of
the rock pile, and Sergeant Madding lay at the foot
of it sighting along his rifle. In a few moments the
Chinese bugler would sound another call to signal
the charge.

It was then that a huge, barrel-chested marine
named Gallagher suddenly burst out of the scrub
on that finger of land and up the ridge to the 2nd
platoon. He was the first of the reinforcements to
break through the Chinese fire, and he carried with
him a machine gun and two boxes of ammunition—
the normal load for two men.

Gallagher threw himself down on the ridge next to Lieutenant Yancey. Quickly, surely, he placed a belt of ammunition in his gun, slammed down the breech-cover, pulled a side lever once, then again so that the gun was primed and ready to fire. No sooner had he finished than the Chinese bugler blew his shrill blasts.

On came the Chinese soldiers, confident, charging in a mass over the edge of the ridge forty yards away, screaming "Marines, you die!" Gallagher waited, stretched prone behind his gun. Then, as he squeezed the trigger, he swung the weapon from side to side. The other marines fired too until their ammunition was gone. Only Gallagher could keep going.

Unaware that Gallagher had arrived with his precious gun, the Chinese were caught helpless on top of the ridge. They crumpled over, riddled. More kept coming. More fell. The burst from Gallagher's gun made a sustained roar at first. Then the intervals between them gradually grew longer, as fewer Chinese dared rush over the edge of the ridge. Finally the bursts stopped altogether and silence settled over Hill 698.

Shortly after, the 1st platoon of Company E got through to the ridge, and Hill 698 was soon bristling with rifles and machine guns. A second Chinese counterattack came, led by a major, but Yancey and his men could rest as the squads of the 1st platoon mowed the enemy down. Lieutenant Clements, the 1st platoon's commander, leaned over the edge of the ridge. Then, holding onto a tree trunk with his left hand and aiming his carbine with his right, he shot the Chinese major through the head.

Before nightfall Hill 698 was permanently won. In the scrub around it and along its slopes lay many Chinese dead. But on the top of the ridge, where the thirty-two men of the 2nd platoon had fought, there were more than a hundred of them.

Now all along the ridge came the sounds of frozen earth being hacked and dug, of scuffling feet and muttered commands as Company E took up its positions for the night.

In the days that followed there were more fights along the ridges near Sudong in North Korea. There were bitter skirmishes and pulverizing artillery duels in which thousands of Chinese were killed. But the enemy defenses broke, and the 7th Regiment prepared to push on to the north. So it began to gather itself up from the ridges.

Company E with its 2nd platoon and Lieutenant Yancey—his burnt hand trussed up in a bandage—

were ordered down to the road. Along with other companies and platoons, they were formed into a column which headed up into the dark valley and the icy mountain passes. Ahead of them lay more battles—at river crossings, on the ridges and ravines, and in the villages. It was destined that the 2nd platoon of Company E was to fight far up in the north along the frozen waters of a reservoir, an action even more desperate than its assault on Hill 698.

Day after day, the marines of the 7th Regiment trudged up the valley into the snows and winds. In their coats with pointed hoods they looked like helmeted men-of-arms in olden times.

And with them trudged other columns of men who marched unseen and unheard. They marched to rolling drums and screeching fifes. Led by officers in powdered wigs, they marched in black boots and gaiters and hats with jaunty cockades. They marched in green coats with white cross belts, in deep blue ones with gold-trimmed belts, in dark green, in mud-spattered brown, or in sweaty, sun-bleached khaki. They were the marines of ten wars and more than 200 battles already fought and won but never forgotten—of raids on enemy coasts; engagements at sea on the decks of proud frigates; countless skirmishes, storming parties and landings in far-off places. They were the men who had made and handed down all the traditions that lay behind that trudging column in the valley, traditions of things endured and things accomplished.

The Continentals

2

IN MILITARY history, the word "marine" is an old term. As long ago as 500 B.C. the Greeks carried marines on their galleys to lead boarding parties that surged over the rails and onto the decks of enemy vessels. Many other nations have had marines, including France, Russia, Italy, Austria, and Japan. But the direct ancestors of the United States Marines were the Royal Marines of Great Britain.

Organized in 1664, the Royal Marines were sea-soldiers stationed aboard British men-of-war. In battle they took positions on deck or high up in the rigging and fired their muskets at the crews of enemy ships. The Royal Marines were used also to fight on land, going ashore in long-boats while the gunfire from their ships gave them protection by bombarding the enemy forts.

During the early colonial days, American colonists saw much of the Royal Marines and served with them on expeditions against unfriendly settlements along the North American coast. So, when the War for Independence broke out, it was a natural development for the colonies to have their own corps of sea-soldiers. On November 10th, 1775, the Continental Congress at Philadelphia passed a law which gave the country two new battalions to be known as the Continental Marines.

In the rush of preparing for war, there followed busy days of recruiting in Philadelphia. Fife and drum corps paraded down the cobblestone streets. Adventurous young men were asked to go to Tun's Tavern on the waterfront. There they drank ale and ate steak while they were looked over by the recruiting officers. If they were hardy men who knew about the sea and firearms, they were urged to enlist. Most of them accepted.

The new uniform of the Continental Marines, like the Tavern's ale and steak, was tempting. Enlisted men wore light-colored breeches and green cutaway coats faced with white and decorated with many pewter buttons. The rims of their black leather hats were smartly turned up on one side. Officers were more elegant, with silver buttons on their coats, silver epaulettes, and a three-cornered cocked hat.

By the end of 1775 the Continental Marines were ready to fight. They were commanded by Captain Samuel Nicholas, the first American in the Revolution to become a marine officer. Very few facts about Captain Nicholas have come down to us. It is known, however, that he was a prominent man in Philadelphia where he was born and where his mother ran a tavern. Like many young men at that time he probably spent much of his youth in the honorable pursuit of the sea. An ardent sportsman, he loved to fish, race horses, and ride in the fox hunts held in the rolling countryside near the city.

Upon taking up his command, Captain Nicholas stationed his men aboard the eight ships of the new

Continental Navy whose commodore was Esek Hopkins. Like the Royal Marines, the Continental Marines were responsible for shipboard duties. They helped the ships' captains keep order and discipline, for many crews at that time were a surly lot who had been forced into service unwillingly. Marines became the captains' orderlies, and sentries who guarded the ships' arms chests. They learned also to fire the ships' guns. But it was not long before they took up their duties as soldiers of the sea.

It had been decided by the Congress that the Continental fleet should venture out to challenge the British men-of-war rampaging along the coast. So on January 7th, 1776, Commodore Hopkins' eight ships set sail from Philadelphia.

Shortly after the departure, however, the fleet was beset by troubles. Near the mouth of the Delaware River it was caught in ice jams. When it finally got out to sea, it struck a gale. Two of the vessels collided, forcing one into a South Carolina port.

Discouraged, Commodore Hopkins decided that his crews needed more experience before engaging in battle with British ships of the line. So he headed south, looking for less dangerous prey. He had learned that a valuable supply of guns and gunpowder was stored on the British island of New

Providence in the Bahamas—supplies which George Washington's Continental Army needed badly. The Commodore decided to capture it.

Old Nassau, the capital of New Providence, sat on a hill overlooking an expansive harbor. It was defended by about 200 troops who manned two forts—Fort Montague east of the town and Fort Nassau on the west. As the fleet drew near to the island, Commodore Hopkins and Captain Nicholas made their plans for the first landing action in the history of American marines.

It began on March 2nd far out at sea, out of sight of the island, when 200 marines and fifty sailors, all under Captain Nicholas, were transferred into two small sloops. The sloops bore on ahead of the fleet toward New Providence. The next morning they sailed into the harbor heading for the shore line below Fort Nassau. In the light wind they crept on unchallenged, for the British sentries could see only a few ragged and harmless seamen sprawled on the decks of the sloops. But out of sight in the hold crouched the marines and sailors ready for a surprise attack. Upon reaching shore, these men would charge across the beach and seize the fort before the British redcoats could defend themselves.

As it often happens, unforeseen complications

The marines fight their first action aboard a warship

upset the plans. Hopkins' fleet followed too closely behind the sloops and before they were ready to land, they were seen by the British, whose suspicions were aroused. The cannon at Fort Nassau opened fire on the sloops. But instead of returning to the fleet, Nicholas shifted his course and, braving the British gunfire, landed his men at the eastern end of the island near Fort Montague. With him he carried the first American flag to fly over foreign soil.

Even though Captain Nicholas' first plan had been discovered, the British were caught unaware by his landing. They had left only a few soldiers at Fort Montague and these fired three cannon shots and fled. Captain Nicholas simply marched his men through the thickets and into the fort where they spent a quiet night, bothered only by the relentless heat and the nipping of the mosquitoes.

The next morning, with Fort Montague in American hands and the American Navy sitting brazenly in the harbor, the British decided that defense was useless. Nicholas led his marines and sailors into the old town, captured the Government House, the Governor, and the Lieutenant Governor. At Fort Nassau he seized seventy-one cannon and fifteen brass mortars. But only twenty-four casks of gunpowder could be found. The British, he learned, had secreted 150 casks aboard a merchant ship which had escaped from the harbor the night before. After two weeks ashore, Nicholas returned to the ships with his men and prisoners, and on March 17th the fleet sailed away from New Providence.

Commodore Hopkins set a northerly course, for it was important that he bring home the captured supplies for Washington's under-equipped Army as quickly as possible. For more than two weeks, the eight American ships sailed on with little to disturb them. On April 4th they seized a British schooner. At dawn, April 5th, in sight of Block Island off the Connecticut coast, they captured a brig, and toward dusk, a brigantine and a sloop out of New York. Captain Nicholas, aboard the *Alfred* which was the Commodore's flagship, wrote in his diary: "We had at sunset 12 sail, a very pleasant evening."

But that night, before the morning hours had turned into day, the marines fought their first action aboard warships. Captain Nicholas woke up with the noise of "call to quarters" resounding through the ship. He heard the bosun's whistles, the thumping of feet running up the gangway, and on deck he saw, shaped in the darkness ahead, the billowing

headsails of a strange man-of-war. It was the Britisher *Glasgow*, and she was bearing down on the
lead ship of the American fleet, the brigantine
Cabot.

When the Britisher came within gun range of
her, the *Cabot* fired a broadside. But the *Glasgow*,
a bigger ship with heavier cannon, returned the
broadside with one that was double in weight. Then
another one. The blasts of her guns flamed out over
the water as smoke swirled and parted around her
muzzles and her shot crashed into the *Cabot*.
Canvas ripped; wood splintered; the brigantine
reeled, her decks strewn with wreckage, her captain
wounded, her master and several men killed.

The *Alfred*, meanwhile, was approaching the
Britisher under full sail. As big and well armed as
the *Glasgow*, she loosed a broadside into the enemy
ship. The *Glasgow* retaliated.

Aboard the *Alfred* the marines began picking off
the British crew with their long muskets. The
Royal Marines fired back.

The battle raged on for thirty minutes as the
two ships maneuvered, often firing their cannon as
close as pistol range. But the greater experience of
the British began to tell. One of their broadsides
carried away the *Alfred's* wheel ropes and blocks so

that she could not be steered—a helpless target for the *Glasgow's* cannon. Shells struck the *Alfred* below the water line; her mainmast was shot through; up in the tops, spars dangled crazily in the stays. As she was pummeled, her seamen worked desperately on the steering mechanism and after many perilous minutes put it in working order.

Now the *Alfred* could fight back on equal terms. But the British captain, seeing other American ships closing in on his ship as fast as the wind would carry them, began to disengage from the battle. His ship, too, was battered. Ten shot had smashed into her mainmast. Two hundred and fifty more had cut her rigging to pieces, leaving gaping holes in her canvas. She sent up signals for the British fleet lying nearby at Rhode Island to come to her aid. Then she bore off with the wind behind her, as the American ships tailed hard after.

Now, aboard the *Alfred*, Commodore Hopkins, a thoughtful and deliberate man, faced a knotty problem. He weighed it carefully. Should he continue the pursuit up the coast and risk, for the sake of capturing one vessel, a major engagement with the entire British fleet? Or should he put in to port and deliver the captured ships and war-stores safely ashore? At 6:30 A.M. the Commodore made his decision. He signaled his fleet to haul by the wind and leave off the chase.

On April 8th Hopkins delivered his prizes and war-stores at New London, Connecticut. Twenty-four men had been killed or wounded in the fight with the *Glasgow*, seventeen of them Marines.

During the remaining years of the War for Independence, Captain Nicholas, promoted to major, served ashore as the first Commandant of the marines. Some of his men were attached to George Washington's army.

Other marines went to sea. They raided British ports and fought in twelve naval actions against British men-of-war. In a battle off Flamborough Head, England, between Captain John Paul Jones' *Bonhomme Richard* and the British *Serapis*, marines and sailors took positions on yard arms and on perches along the masts. Armed with muskets and grenades, they rained havoc upon the British ship. Their shooting was so accurate that when the battle had reached its full height, the quarter deck of the *Serapis* was littered with bodies and no Englishman dared even to venture out on it.

One grenade thrown from the rigging helped turn the tide in favor of the *Bonhomme Richard.*

It struck the side of a hatchway, rebounded crazily, and dropped into a powder magazine.

"The effect," wrote Lieutenant Dale, Captain Jones' first lieutenant, "was tremendous; more than twenty of the enemy were blown to pieces, and many stood with only the collars of their shirts upon their bodies."

By the end of the war in 1783, all but one of the ships in the Continental Navy had been sunk or captured. The last vessel, the *Alliance,* was sold. With no Navy left and with the country devoting its efforts to peaceful pursuits, the Continental Marines were disbanded. Major Samuel Nicholas went back to a seafaring life on merchant ships. Finally, tiring of this, he settled down in Philadelphia, fishing, racing horses, and running the tavern his mother had left him.

Tripoli and a Sword

3

THE UNITED STATES soon decided to re-build its Navy. Pirates from the Barbary Coast of North Africa were preying on American ship-ping and trouble was brewing with an old ally, France.

Since the Revolution, France had come to re-gard America almost as her property. Now that the French were at war with the British, the French were using neutral American waters to carry on campaigns against their enemy. They even went so far as to capture American merchant ships to help support their fleet.

In May 1798, after diplomacy had failed to stop these activities, Congress lost its patience and ordered its Navy to fight the French. In July, 1798, it reestablished the Continental Marines—this time as the United States Marine Corps—to consist of thirty-three officers and 848 enlisted men.

The marines of this period performed the same duties as the Continentals, but their uniforms were more colorful. Their shortcoats and trousers were blue, edged in brilliant red, while their hats, still turned up on the side, were decorated with a yellow band and cockade. Sergeants wore yellow epaulettes on their shoulders. Officers had long blue coats with red cuffs and golden epaulettes. But all ranks wore stiff leather collars which earned for the marines the nickname "Leathernecks."

The new Commandant of the Corps was Major William Burrows of South Carolina, a veteran of the Revolution. Burrows was a courtly but determined man, who began to build the prestige of the young service. He persuaded Congress to increase its size to more than 1,000 men. He procured a headquarters building. To advertise the Corps, he formed the Marine Band—the country's first national band.

At the inauguration of Thomas Jefferson, the marines boomed out a rousing new tune which was called "Jefferson's March." It had been written specially for the occasion. The new President was delighted and from then on regarded the band as his own corps of musicians, asking it to play at many private as well as state ceremonies. Ever since Jefferson's day, the Marine Band has been known as the "President's Own."

In later years, the band rose to national prominence under the leadership of John Philip Sousa, the great bandmaster. Under him, the band in its gold-braided coats toured the country many times. Sousa, an accomplished composer, wrote many marches for the marines. One of them, among his most famous, he called "Semper Fidelis"—the Latin motto inscribed on the marine flag. It means "Always faithful."

Burrows distributed his marines among twenty-five warships. Aboard the frigate *Constitution* he placed a detachment of fifty men under the command of Captain Daniel Carmick, who was soon to take part in the most dashing adventure of the brief French war.

In May, 1800, the *Constitution* was prowling through the Caribbean when she discovered a French corvette, the *Sandwich*, sitting in the harbor of Porto Plata, Santo Domingo. The corvette was taking on a cargo of sugar and coffee and would make a rich prize.

Porto Plata was a Spanish settlement, but Silas Talbot, Captain of the *Constitution*, could not resist an attempt to capture the Frenchman even though she lay in neutral waters. He placed Carmick with forty marines and Lieutenant Isaac Hull with forty sailors aboard a tiny sloop named the *Sally*. On the evening of May 11th the *Sally* sailed for Porto Plata, as innocent looking above decks as the sloops that took Captain Nicholas and his marines into New Providence.

For twelve hours the marines and sailors sat in the sweltering hold of the *Sally*. About midnight, halfway to Porto Plata, a man-of-war intercepted her, firing warning shots across her bow. The sloop hove to. Had she fallen into a French trap?

A longboat came alongside and a tall figure heading a party of armed men climbed out of the shadows and over the *Sally's* gunwale. As he walked under the dim light of the ship's lanterns, the scarlet of his coat glowed warmly across his shoulders. Lieutenant Hull, waiting to receive him, saw then with a sigh of relief that the stranger was a British officer.

Hull explained the *Sally's* mission.

"Well, good luck," replied the English officer in a disappointed tone. "We have been watching that Frenchman. We were going to capture her when she came out of port."

"When she comes out of port," said Hull, "she will be my prize."

Porto Plata lay quiet in the noon sun when the *Sally* sailed in and edged up to the French corvette under the guns of the Spanish fort that commanded the harbor. The decks of the *Sandwich* were deserted, her crew apparently enjoying their Sunday dinner below. In Captain Carmick's own words, the men went aboard the French ship "like devils."

Totally surprised, the French crew offered no more resistance than a few scattered musket shots. With the ship taken, Carmick and his marines rowed ashore in the corvette's boats. They seized the Spanish fort at Porto Plata, disabled its guns, and returned to the *Sandwich*—all within the remarkably short time of thirty minutes.

It remained now to make the corvette ready to sail, for her top masts were down and her canvas

Lieutenant O'Bannon raises the first American flag to fly over a fortress of the Old World

was furled. By 6:00 P.M. she was rigged. But the wind had failed.

Meanwhile the town defenders, unable to use their cannon in the fort and unwilling to attack the alerted Americans by long-boats, sent emissaries with flags of truce and bargaining propositions. Carmick and Hull refused to negotiate and at two o'clock the next morning, when the wind had freshened, they sailed their prize from the harbor unmolested.

The exploit was admired by everyone. However, the authorities in Washington were forced to admit that it was unlawful. Silas Talbot had been wrong in attacking a neutral Spanish fort. Later, the *Sandwich* was returned to the French.

When the naval war with France ended in 1801, the United States faced difficulties on the North African coast. The Bashaw (ruler) of Tripoli had been one of the haughtiest and most troublesome of the Barbary pirates. He had raided American shipping. He had demanded—and received—ransom money for the return of his captives and tribute money for permission to sail in Tripolitan waters. But year after year he had demanded larger and

larger sums until the United States Congress refused to pay. So on May 10, 1801, the Bashaw
declared war.

The United States waged a haphazard naval
campaign against the Bashaw until 1803, when it
sent a fleet of eight ships to blockade the port of
Tripoli. On October 31st one of these ships, the
Philadelphia, gave chase to a Tripolitan vessel near
the African shore and ran aground. Frantically, her
crew strove to free her but she was stuck fast.
Pirate gunboats swarming out from Tripoli captured the helpless American frigate, stripped the
marines and sailors of their belongings and took
them, half-naked, into the prisons of the town.

In time the Tripolitans dislodged the *Philadelphia.* They remounted her guns and moored her in
Tripoli harbor where the Bashaw could see his
handsome prize. But she did not remain handsome
for long.

On the night of February 16, 1804, an American
naval lieutenant named Stephen Decatur of the
Constitution took a volunteer party of sailors and
marines aboard a tiny ketch, the *Intrepid.* The
ketch swung around toward the shore and slipped
through the darkness into the harbor of Tripoli.

She stole through the enemy gunboats and cruisers up to the side of the *Philadelphia*. Before the astonished Tripolitans manning the captured ship could fight back, they were overpowered by Decatur's sailors and marines, silently pouring over the side with cutlasses in their teeth. The Americans set fire to the *Philadelphia* and disappeared into the *Intrepid* as suddenly as they had come.

As the flames shot up into the sky, the harbor awoke. But the *Intrepid* sailed through the confusion of Tripolitan shouts, of canvas hoisted into place, of cannon futilely discharged. She got away safely as the *Philadelphia* burned to a charred ruin under the muzzles of pirate guns and under the eyes of the enraged Bashaw.

The blockade of Tripoli continued. On August 3rd, 1804, the American fleet began a bombardment of the city, and at the same time, American gunboats sailed into the harbor.

Despite this the Bashaw of Tripoli held out stubbornly. Obviously, it was necessary to attack him on the land as well as on the sea. A plan had been suggested to President Jefferson by General William Eaton, an American official at Tunis who had had much experience in the Near East.

Eaton wanted to hire the Bashaw's brother, Hamet Karamanli, who himself had once been the ruler of Tripoli. He had been driven from the throne by his brother and had been forced to seek refuge in Egypt. Eaton felt sure that with American help Hamet could be persuaded to lead a revolt against the Bashaw. Agreeing to the scheme, President Jefferson, in the autumn of 1804, sent Eaton to Egypt to begin negotiations.

Hamet, remembering his fine days as Bashaw of Tripoli, was willing to cooperate. At a camp near Alexandria, Eaton recruited an army. It was a rabble of mercenaries—soldiers who will fight under any flag for pay. Among them were Greeks, Spaniards, Germans, Italians, Levantines—plus asses, camels, and unruly Hamet-led Arabs. Eaton intended to lead this strange army across the desert of Barca and strike first at Derne, a Tripolitan seaport. Then, as the rebellion spread and Hamet gathered armed support from his countrymen, he would move on Tripoli itself. To discipline and serve as an example for his motley army, Eaton had with him eight United States Marines—six privates, one sergeant, and a young lieutenant from Virginia named Presley O'Bannon.

O'Bannon was a gay, reckless officer. He would charm the ladies ashore, and aboard ship would amuse his companions with his fiddle.

On March 8, 1805, the army set out across the desert to Bomba, its first stopping place. There it was to be met by American ships bringing supplies for the advance on Derne. From the beginning of its trek, the expedition was almost overcome by difficulties. Even on the first evening the camel drivers demanded their pay in advance and mutinied. Eaton had to call on the mercenaries to put up a show of force that persuaded the drivers to keep going.

As the army pushed on, it was joined by bands of Arabs until it numbered 1000 men. But again and again, the Arabs would refuse to march, demanding more money for their services. To bluff them into moving, Eaton would line up the marines and mercenaries and threaten to shoot the Arabs down if they did not march on ahead with the others. At last the Arabs, sulking and ashamed, would trail along behind.

Four days from Bomba, the last of the rations were eaten and a camel had to be slaughtered. The army staggered on parched, blistered, starved and on April 15th it reached the port. But the haven of food

and water it had expected was nowhere to be found
—only the bleak desert town on the rocks of the
coast. Nor was there a ship in sight. The expedition
was on the verge of collapse when at eight o'clock the
next morning a sail came over the horizon. It was the
Argus, loaded with provisions.

The march went on as Eaton and O'Bannon led
their reluctant, shambling army to Derne, 120 miles
away. The American General sent a note to the Bey
of the city demanding that he surrender. Loyal to
the Bashaw, the Bey retorted with surprising blunt-
ness for an Arab: "My head or yours."

Two days later Eaton decided to attack. Three
United States warships sailed into the harbor to
bombard the city while Hamet and his Arabs were
sent to make an assault from the south. O'Bannon,
at the head of the marines and mercenaries, was
placed in a line facing the fort of Derne.

The battle broke with the booming of the naval
bombardment. Soon the gun and musket fire from
both sides was heavy. But the Tripolitans began to
concentrate their shooting on O'Bannon's force. As
the increasing enemy fire crackled into the sand
around them, the mercenaries began to show signs
of panic. Many of them broke into confusion. Eaton

and O'Bannon tried to restore order, but their efforts were useless.

In a desperate measure, General Eaton ordered a charge. The marines and a few of the mercenaries responded to his command, a scattering of men rushing forward against many times their number. Leading them, Eaton was struck in the wrist by a musket ball.

O'Bannon took over, carrying the assault into a hail of Tripolitan musketry fired from the fort and the walls of houses. Three marines fell, and several Greeks. But the handful of men could not be stopped by an enemy that had never before encountered such headlong tactics. Startled at first, then caught off-balance as the marines were suddenly among them, the Tripolitans ran back from wall to wall, palm tree to palm tree, finally yielding their fort and battery of guns to O'Bannon and his men.

By 4 P.M. the Bey's palace had fallen and the city was taken. Over the fort at Derne an American flag waved in a gentle breeze raised there by Marine Lieutenant O'Bannon—the first American flag to fly over a fortress of the Old World.

Thus the first phase of Eaton's plan had been accomplished. It now remained to gather additional support for Hamet and to advance on Tripoli. But the campaign was never fought. On June 3rd Eaton, still at Derne, received dispatches that the United States had signed a peace treaty with the Bashaw of Tripoli, agreeing to pay him a ransom of $60,000 for the return of the prisoners captured on the *Philadelphia*. Eaton was embittered by the news. He was convinced that with a reinforcement of a hundred marines he could have overthrown the Bashaw and taught him a lesson for his piracy. No doubt such a treaty should not have been signed. It seemed to reveal weakness in the United States rather than strength, and it seemed to condone piracy rather than to punish it.

The American Congress passed a resolution praising the "patriotism, intrepidity and valor" of both O'Bannon and Eaton. On December 26, 1805, the Virginia House of Delegates presented O'Bannon with a beautiful Mameluk sword designed after one which Hamet had given him as a token of his gratitude.

Inexcusably, the Marine Corps itself did not at first give O'Bannon proper recognition for his part in the Derne campaign. He was commended, but he was not offered a promotion to a captaincy, a fact which caused him to resign in disgust in 1807. Not for many years did the Corps pay him the honor he deserved. When it adopted an official sword for its officers, O'Bannon's was chosen as the model—a finely curving blade with an ivory hilt topped by the head of a golden eagle.

The Exploits of John Gamble

4

THE YEAR 1812 brought with it another war. This time it was the British who raided American merchantmen and who forced American seamen to serve in the English Navy. They were also spreading their control from Canada south over the Great Lakes region and down into fertile American frontier land. The aroused western states urged a declaration of war. It came on June 18th.

During the two and a half years of fighting, the

Marine Corps, now 1300 strong, fought on land and on sea. It added much to its young history—actions which marines themselves talked about and became proud of.

There were grim defeats, too. On June 1, 1813, the *U.S.S. Chesapeake,* commanded by Captain Lawrence, met the *Shannon* in a duel off Boston. At first the *Chesapeake's* broadsides sent the Britisher reeling. But when she herself began to take punishment, some of her poorly disciplined crew deserted their guns in a panic.

Captain Lawrence was wounded and while being carried below to die gave his last—and immortal—instructions: "Don't Give Up the Ship." Many of his sailors did not answer to the command, but fled below when the British boarded the wreckage of the *Chesapeake.*

On the upper decks, however, marines under Lieutenant James Broom held to their stations until all were killed or wounded. They fought from the tops until the *Shannon's* guns cleared them from aloft in a brutal havoc of falling bodies.

The jobs done by the marines went on from battle to battle and place to place, as their traditions began to flower. But there were no exploits in the

records of the Corps to compare with those of a lieutenant named John Marshall Gamble. His adven-
tures began on October 22, 1812 when, in command of thirty-one marines, he set sail with Captain
David Porter on the *Essex*.

Porter made his way to the Pacific Ocean where
he captured three British whalers in the Galápagos
Islands and manned them with American crews.
Though marine officers were not supposed to be able
to sail ships, Porter placed one of his prizes, the
Greenwich, under the command of Lieutenant
Gamble.

One day in July Porter sighted three enemy sails.
His fleet gave chase, and it fell to Lieutenant Gamble to match his seamanship against the Britisher
Seringapatam—the scourge of American whalers in
the vicinity. From the bow of the *Essex*, Captain
Porter watched Gamble's maneuvers with interest,
peering through his spyglass and nervously chewing
a wad of tobacco.

At one point, as the *Greenwich* neared the *Seringapatam*, Porter exclaimed aloud, "Now, Mr.
Gamble, if you'll only stand on course for five minutes and then tack, I'll make you a prince."

That, as it turned out, was exactly what Gamble
did. He intercepted the Britisher, loosed a number

of broadsides into her and forced her to strike her colors.

Autumn came, the ships needed refitting, and there was danger of British cruisers in the vicinity. So Captain Porter put into the Marquesas Islands where he built a base and a fort on the island of Nukuhiva.

Life on that island was never peaceful. The shifty Marquesan natives continually fought among themselves, and on more than one occasion the Americans had to join in the local wars.

By December, 1813, two of the ships were ready to go to sea again. Captain Porter sailed them from the harbor bound for the South American coast, leaving Lieutenant Gamble behind with twenty-one men and the remaining three ships. Porter's instructions to him had an ominous sound—he was to hold the base at Nukuhiva until Porter returned. In the event that Porter did not return, Gamble was to hold the base for five and a half months.

Porter never came back. Trapped at Valparaiso by two British men-of-war, he was forced to surrender.

As the days passed at Nukuhiva, Gamble found himself enclosed by an ever-tightening ring of treachery. The natives, realizing that he now had

The Americans pulled hard for the nearest of the ships

only a handful of marines and sailors, began to steal his provisions. Some of his own men had struck up friendships with native girls, were giving them precious food, and permitting them to swim out to the ships. Four of the men even deserted with a valuable supply of powder and muskets.

By April, it was almost time to leave Nukuhiva, and as the day of departure drew near, Gamble's men grew more sullen. They loafed at their work and many times he caught them watching him closely. On May 7, aboard the *Seringapatam,* they attacked him, bound his hands and feet and threw him into the brig. One of the mutineers fired a pistol at him as he lay helpless on the floor, and the ball pierced his heel. Those who remained loyal to him —Midshipmen Feltus, Clapp, and a few others— were thrown in after him.

The mutineers set sail in the *Seringapatam.* Four miles out they gave Gamble and his men three old muskets, put them into a leaky boat, and then headed off to sea. In constant danger of being swamped, Gamble and his party managed to row back to the base at Nukuhiva only to find greater trouble awaiting them.

The natives, having heard of the mutiny, plundered the Americans' stores. In a fierce skirmish on the beach, they massacred four of Gamble's men, including Midshipman Feltus. Driven across the sand to the water's edge, the Americans jumped into a boat, pulling hard for the nearest of the ships, the *Sir Andrew Hammond*. The Marquesans scrambled into their long, pointed canoes and swarmed out into the harbor after them. The Americans reached the ship, but the natives pressed on.

Aboard the *Sir Andrew Hammond* Gamble ran to the guns which he always kept loaded. Hobbling from one to the other on his wounded foot, he fired them at the native craft until they scurried back out of range.

Gamble's crew consisted now of only three sailors and three marines. Quickly they hoisted the sails and soon were out of the fatal harbor.

The Americans had no map, spyglass or compass, but trade winds carried them for fifteen days until they came to the Hawaiian Islands where they found shelter with friendly natives. There they heard of a ship seen recently off the islands whose description tallied with that of the *Seringapatam*. Gamble decided to go after her and bring the mutineers to justice. But while sailing among the Islands in search of provisions, he encountered the British man-of-war, *Cherub*. Defenseless with his small crew, he surrendered and was taken to Valparaiso as a prisoner. When the war ended he was released, finally to return home where rapid promotions to major and lieutenant colonel awaited him.

Thirty-nine Years Under Archibald Henderson

AFTER THE war of 1812, the marines felt the dullness of peacetime routine. The detachments scattered here and there began to fret with boredom. Discipline was slackened, and the morale of the men suffered.

This is a lethargy that can overtake any fighting organization in peacetime unless it has good leadership to keep it alert and busy. And the marine leadership at the time was far from good. The steps made by Commandant Burrows to build the Corps virtually crumbled under his successor, Major Franklin Wharton. In fact, Wharton had behaved disgracefully when the British invaded Washington. Instead of leading his marines against the enemy, he fled from the city with his paymaster.

Wharton died in 1818 but his successor, Lieutenant Colonel Anthony Gale, was no better. A stubborn man, Gale quarreled with the Secretary of the Navy, with his own officers and became, after little more than a year, an objectionable drunkard. He was arrested, court-martialed, and dismissed from the service.

With another Commandant like Wharton or Gale, the Corps might have completely fallen apart. But Gale's successor was a fiery, red-headed little man named Lieutenant Colonel Archibald Henderson who came from a proud old Virginia family. His father had been a member of the House of Burgesses and a close friend of George Washington.

Henderson stirred up a whirlwind. He inspected the detachments, striding erect and immaculate before the lines of marines. He founded a school where officers were trained under his personal supervision. He standardized the uniform which many marines had changed to suit themselves. And he demanded the most rigid discipline. Punishments could be severe in those days and Henderson saw that they were doled out liberally to those who deserved them. Usually, the offenders were lashed with the cat-o'-nine-tails, chained in the "brig," or made to walk their posts for hours carrying heavy cannon balls or wearing big iron collars. If their offenses were serious enough they were drummed out of the Corps. When that happened, the culprit stood before a formation of marines. His offense was formally read out, his insignia ripped from his uniform. Then he was led off the post in disgrace between two long lines of marines while drums rolled out the beat that banished him from the service.

Henderson revived the spirit and discipline of the marines. He also gave the Corps a new and challenging mission—to be the "first to fight," ready at all times to sally forth against an enemy wherever in the world the enemy may strike. His doctrine became fundamental in the Corps which, to the present day, has tried to live up to it.

For thirty-nine years Archibald Henderson served as Commandant. He served during a fearless age, when America threw itself into the world-wide competition for trade, prestige and power. So, for Henderson's marines, it was a busy age. It saw them fighting pirates in the West Indies and in tortuous hideouts along the Florida coast. It saw them landing at Foxardo, Puerto Rico, seizing a fort, and exacting from the pirate chief a personal apology for insulting an American naval officer. It saw them—this time on the other side of the globe—storming ashore at Quallah Batto, Sumatra, destroying towns in retaliation for the robbing of an American merchant ship.

The marines were also called on to put down troubles at home. One incident, talked of for years, occurred in 1824. At the Massachusetts State Prison in Boston, 283 prisoners broke out of their cells. They had been infuriated by a prison order sentencing three of them to be whipped. Armed with knives, clubs and hammers stolen from the prison workshop, they gathered in the dining hall. There the dangerous, growling mob informed the prison officials that they would not submit until the sentences were commuted.

The officials called Major Robert Wainwright, commander of the marines at the Boston Navy Yard. When he arrived with only thirty men, he was advised to stay out of the dining hall and shoot at the criminals through the windows. This, the Major decided, would bring unnecessary bloodshed. He ordered the dining-hall door thrown open.

Tall, straight, he marched in at the head of his men and lined them up at one end of the room facing the mob at the other end. He addressed the convicts. The marines, he told them, would not leave the hall until every convict had returned to his duty. The replies, defiant and jeering, rolled back down the length of the hall.

Wainwright's voice cracked like a whip as he ordered his men to load their rifles. But the convicts showed no fear, realizing, as did Wainwright himself, that after the first discharge they could overrun the marines before the next volley could be fired. Again the Major's command snapped out. His men took aim. The convicts grasped their weapons tighter, and a silence hung over the room.

It was broken as Wainwright spoke again, urging the convicts to leave peacefully. They refused, more defiantly and confidently this time. With their muskets leveled, the marines waited for the command to fire. But again the Major turned to the convicts. "You must leave this hall," he said. "I give you three minutes to decide. If at the end of that time a man remains, he shall be shot dead. I speak no more."

Not a muscle moved in the room. Not a sound was heard as the whole prison became aware of the suspense of the moment. Glaring down the shadowy hall into the muzzles of the muskets, the convicts measured their strength against the handful of marines who looked maddeningly blank and unperturbed. Wainwright's eyes were fixed coldly on his watch. The seconds went by until two minutes had almost passed.

From the ranks of the convicts now came the sounds of tense breathing, barely audible at first and gradually swelling into a rasp of fury and fear. From the rear of the mob two men slowly walked toward the nearest door. A few others followed quietly, deliberately, and then faster. Suddenly panic gripped the prisoners. They crowded, shuffled, and surged for the exit. Before the last half-minute was gone, the great dining hall lay empty before the sighted gaze of the marines.

In 1836 Commandant Henderson had his chance to demonstrate that his marines were, as he had planned, a ready fighting force. A war with the Indians had flared up in Florida. As was usually the case in these wars, white men wanted Indian land. Two years before the Creek and Cherokee tribes of

Georgia and the Seminoles of Florida had made a treaty with the American government. In the treaty, the Indians agreed to turn their land over to the white men and move to reservations west of the Mississippi.

The Seminoles, however, refused to live up to the agreement and went on the warpath. The Creeks joined them, and Georgia and Florida were rampaged by Indian raids. Roanoke was burned to the ground, and as the revolt spread, the Army, with only a thousand men in the southeast, was hard-pressed to keep order. So Henderson volunteered the marines.

President Andrew Jackson accepted the offer. Thereupon Henderson, bubbling over with energy and the prospect of a fight, stripped the marine detachments of half their numbers. With these men he formed two battalions and took command of them himself. He left an aging sergeant major in charge of his office in Washington and tacked a sign on the door: "Gone to Florida to fight the Indians. Will be back when the war is over."

On arriving in Augusta, Georgia, Henderson received his combat orders from the Army commander, General Jessup. In ten days he marched his battalions 224 miles to the Chattahoochee River in the country of the Creeks. There he waged a campaign in the malaria-ridden swamps of the river. It was only a matter of weeks before the Creeks were forced to sue for peace.

Commandant Henderson was put in command of a combined Army-Marine Brigade which he marched into the Florida Everglades to fight the Seminoles. He suffered many losses in the ambushes lurking along the trails that fingered into the swamps. But he drove his force on, and the retreating Seminoles were finally compelled to make a stand on the Hatchee Lustee River.

The river was broad, swift, and could not be waded. Henderson spread some of his men along the bank to fire at the Indians on the other side. The remaining men felled trees that were used to span the river. Marines dashed across the precarious bridges. Some of them even swam the current. Those who got through the Indian musketry covered the crossing of the rest of the brigade. The Seminoles retired quickly, but Henderson pressed after them, destroying their blankets, clothing and baggage. It was then January, 1837. By the spring the Seminoles had agreed to move west, and the war, apparently, was over.

Henderson returned to Washington, and his marines later went back to the stations from which they had come. No sooner had the Americans weakened themselves than the Seminoles took to the warpath again. For five more years the sporadic campaign went on. This time the marines were attached to the Navy. They manned a "mosquito fleet" of canoes and barges which they poled and paddled up the streams deep into Indian country, intercepting Seminole supplies and making raids on their camps.

The Indians, stubborn and proud, took defeat after defeat until they withdrew to an almost unassailable position in the heart of Florida's Everglades. There, in a tract of land no white man wanted, they were allowed to remain.

During his long term at the head of the marines —the longest of any Commandant — Archibald Henderson served under eight Presidents. It was under President Polk that his marines became involved in the American conquest of California and the war with Mexico. Both campaigns were the results of America's ambition to spread out over the southwest and western regions of a continent it considered its own.

In March, 1845 the United States annexed Texas, an act which left the Mexicans embittered. Next, President Polk decided to acquire the territory of New Mexico as well and began negotiations with the Mexicans to purchase it.

The President also wanted California which, like New Mexico, was under Mexican domination. The English too had their eyes on California, and their warships were known to be hovering around the Pacific seaports.

In October, 1845 Polk decided to send a message to three important men in California: his consul at Monterey, Thomas O. Larkin; the commander of the Navy's Pacific squadron, Commodore Sloat; and the famous pathfinder and soldier, John C. Fremont, then leading an exploring expedition in northern California. The message instructed these men to scheme to separate California from Mexico and to arouse in the settlers of California a love of liberty and a distrust for the British. To carry this vital dispatch across Mexico to California, Polk selected a young lieutenant of the marines named Archibald A. Gillespie who spoke Spanish fluently and who, like his fiery Commandant, had a shock of flaming red hair.

Lieutenant Gillespie rallying his men

Gillespie memorized the President's message, destroyed it in case the Mexicans should capture him, and disguised himself as a salesman for a Scottish whiskey firm, MacDougal Distilleries of Edinburgh. Setting out in November, he went by boat to Vera Cruz. By liberally handing out pesos, he passed through the customs and without once arousing suspicion, reached Mexico City in a month. In a stagecoach he travelled to the port of Mazatlan on the Pacific coast. In the harbor lay an American sloop of war, the *Cyane*, and a British ship of the line, the *Collingwood*, which was obviously there to promote British interests.

It was urgent that Gillespie reach Monterey (and Consul Larkin) farther north as soon as possible. That night he slipped aboard the *Cyane*. After a hurried conference, her commander, Captain William Mervine, agreed to take Gillespie to Monterey. To deceive the watchful British admiral aboard the *Collingwood* as to his true destination, Mervine would sail first to Honolulu, offering to take the Britisher's mail there. The British admiral, successfully deceived, agreed happily to the arrangement.

On April 17, 1846, the *Cyane* sailed into Monterey and Gillespie delivered the President's message to Consul Larkin. Somewhere between Mazatlan and Monterey (at sea or at Honolulu), he had already given the dispatch to Commodore Sloat.

Now it remained to find Fremont, who had led his exploring party beyond California into the forests of Oregon. For almost a month Gillespie trailed him up the Sacramento River in a small boat, then over lonely trails on horseback.

On May 9th, 1846, along the southern shore of Klamath Lake, in a wild setting of great, shadowy trees, Gillespie completed his remarkable mission. His meeting with Fremont was an historic event in the growth of the West. The words the young lieutenant recited to the grizzled soldier mapped the destiny of all California as an American territory.

From then on events moved swiftly. A revolt of American settlers in California sprang up and proclaimed the "Bear Flag" Republic. Then came the long-expected news that negotiations with Mexico had failed, and the war was on.

Gillespie became a captain in a mounted battalion of American frontiersmen mobilized and led by Fremont. It was a fierce band of men in buckskin, with beards and untrimmed hair trailing out from under their foraging caps, with long rifles, revolving pistols, and knives in their belts. They struck swiftly, riding out of the hills in the north and capturing Monterey. San Francisco fell too; then San Pedro and Los Angeles.

Lieutenant Gillespie was given a command in the south where he took part in some of the severest fighting. At San Diego he was besieged by a force which swelled to 600 men as the siege progressed. At the same time, the numbers of his own men dropped from seventy-two to fifty-five.

Gillespie held out against four attacks, driving off the Californians with old cannon which he mounted on ox carts. His only ammunition were scraps from blacksmith shops—nails and lead pipe contributed by the owner of a local vineyard. But his defense was so determined that the enemy was thankful to allow him to withdraw with his men, weapons, and supplies intact.

Later, at the battle of San Pasquale, Gillespie fought with the United States Dragoons commanded by Colonel Kearney. The Californians buckled under the weight of the American cavalry. A force of forty dragoons gave chase, but the Californians suddenly wheeled around and stood fast. The dragoon captain was pierced by eight lances, his men thrown into confusion.

At that moment, Gillespie galloped up on his

horse and bellowed, "Rally men, rally men, for God's sake, rally! Show a front, don't turn your backs. Face them, face them!"

With that he charged into the enemy center. He leaned forward to dodge a lance thrown at him, but a blow struck him from behind, hurling him from his horse. A sword cut him to the lung under his left arm, and a fist cracked him in the mouth, bruising his upper lip and knocking out a tooth. He got up and with blood pouring out of the gash in his side, hacked his way to the dragoons who had now rallied. They were grouped around a howitzer, but no one had a match to fire it. Reeling and about to faint, Gillespie fumbled in his clothes for a match he knew was there and set off the gun. The Californians decided to continue their retreat.

The action at San Pasquale took place December 6, 1846. Later in the month 600 marines, sailors, and dragoons advanced from the south to attack Los Angeles, now in the hands of the main enemy force under General Flores. In January 1847 Gillespie, his side still bandaged, fought again in the assault on Los Angeles. He was wounded again too —a carbine bullet in the hip. But he had the strength, the next day, to hoist the American flag over the Los Angeles Government House with his own hands. The capture of the city ended the campaign; the remnants of Flores' troops were fleeing to Mexico and California belonged to America.

While California was being conquered, the war with Mexico proper had gone ahead successfully.

On March 9, 1847, an army under General Winfield Scott seized the port of Vera Cruz. From there Scott marched inland toward Mexico City. The Mexicans pulled back before him, but at Puebla he was held up, not by the enemy, but by a military oddity. The enlistment time of many of his soldiers had expired, so they went home, and Scott was forced to wait for men to replace them.

Back in Washington, meanwhile, Commandant Henderson had been busy. He had obtained from Congress authorization to increase the Marine Corps by 1,000 men. Seeing in Scott's dilemma another chance for marines to fight, he plunged the Corps into a fever of recruiting. As fast as the recruits came, they were sent to Fort Hamilton, New York, and forwarded into a battalion of 300 men under Lieutenant Colonel Samuel Watson.

This battalion was rushed to join Scott's army where it was attached to General John A. Quitman's 4th Division. With the 2nd Pennsylvania Volunteers it constituted a brigade which was placed under the command of Watson. Thus, command of the battalion itself fell to a stocky, square-jawed veteran of the Indian wars, Major Levi Twiggs.

On August 8, 1847, Scott, with his army of 10,738 men, began to move toward Mexico City sixty miles away, site of the palace of the ancient Aztec King, Montezuma. It was a risky undertaking. In attacking the city defenses, Scott's army would be outnumbered three to one. He would be deep in the enemy country, and should he be beaten, retreat would be impossible.

Chapultepec was the main defense before Mexico City. A huge mass of volcanic rock, it commanded the causeways spanning the marshes which led into Mexico City. On top of Chapultepec stood a solid stone castle housing a military school—the West Point of Mexico. The castle was surrounded by a wall, while below it, the rocky hill sheered down to the plain in a drop of some 200 feet which, in places, was almost perpendicular.

At its base, the hill was encircled by another wall

fifteen feet high. The massive rock bristled with fortifications manned by a garrison of 1,000 men and a scattering of military cadets.

Studying the heights, Scott and his commanders pondered how to take the fortress. Quitman's division, they decided, would attack the southern slope where a road wound up the face of the rock. Another division under General Pillow would attack the western slope where the rise was not so steep but was heavily defended. The walls presented the most dangerous problem. Too thick to be battered down entirely by artillery, they would have to be stormed in great strength, with the troops scaling them by ladders.

During the night of September 11, 1847, American siege guns were hauled into position and columns of troops filed along the roads to their attack stations. With the first glimmer of dawn, the bombardment began—eight- and eleven-inch shells crashing into the stone walls of Chapultepec. At 8 A.M. of the 13th the assault troops moved out.

Leading Quitman's division was a storming party of 425 men, including Major Twiggs and his marines. Carrying the heavy unwieldy ladders, they went up the road that curled along the face of the rock. Musket balls, grape shot, and canister rained down on them. Major Twiggs and many others were killed, but the assault waves gained the foot of the wall at the top of the hill, and behind them came the rest of the division.

The spindly ladders were thrown up against the wall. Pushed back by the Mexicans, some of the ladders wobbled in mid-air and crashed into the rocks with marines and soldiers clinging to the rungs. The fire from above did not abate, but the Americans swarmed up the ladders in a tide which overwhelmed the defenders. They rushed to the castle doors, battered them down, and the fighting raged on through the dark corridors in a hand-to-hand brawl of flashing swords and bayonets.

When the castle was won, General Quitman quickly reorganized his scattered division and pressed up the causeway toward Mexico City. The Mexican troops under General Santa Anna resisted furiously, flinging up road blocks and holding to their emplacements until they were routed out. By dusk, the 4th Division had penetrated into the city.

Meanwhile, another American division under General Worth had moved on the city from a different direction, but by nightfall the two forces had not joined. This left Quitman isolated in what might become a dangerous position.

General Scott suggested that Quitman withdraw and renew the attack in company with Worth in the morning. Quitman replied that unless he was ordered to do so he would not budge. "The Capitol is mine," he said to Captain Baker of the marines. "My brave fellows have conquered it, and by God they shall have it!"

Have it they did. That night Santa Anna withdrew his beaten army from the city which, in the early morning hours, was surrendered to General Scott. While Scott was still eating his breakfast, Quitman took his 4th Division through the streets to the Grand Plaza which lay in the shadow of the Aztec Palace. From the windows and roof tops Mexican civilians glumly watched the procession of Americans.

Unkempt, smeared with mud, the soldiers and marines marched by, led by their disheveled general who had lost a shoe in the mud of the causeway. Before the palace they halted and formed in a ragged line. It was 7 A.M. The commands to present arms rang out over the Plaza as a bullet-shredded American flag was raised above the National

Palace where the ancient halls of Montezuma once stood.

The victory—according to tradition—inspired an unknown marine in Mexico to compose the first stanza of a song. He set it to the music of a tune that was popular in those days, taken from an opera called "Genevieve de Brabant" by the German composer, Jacques Offenbach.

1. From the halls of Mon-te-zu-ma To the shores of Trip-o-li; We fight our coun-try's bat-tles In the air, on land, and sea. First to fight for right and free-dom And to keep our hon-or clean, We are proud to claim the ti-tle Of U-nit-ed States Ma-rine.

Thus the famous marching song was born—The Marine Corps Hymn. At first it was sung and played informally. But it spread through the Corps, and as the years passed, new stanzas were written by other unknown marines to commemorate new battles fought. In 1929 two of these stanzas were added to the original one to form an official version of the Hymn.

Our flag's unfurled to every breeze
From dawn to setting sun;
We have fought in ev'ry clime and place
Where we could take a gun;
In the snow of far-off Northern lands
And in sunny tropic scenes;
You will find us always on the job —
The United States Marines.

Here's health to you and to our Corps
Which we are proud to serve;
In many a strife we've fought for life
And never lost our nerve;
If the Army and the Navy
Ever look on Heaven's scenes;
They will find the streets are guarded
By United States Marines.

In 1942 the marines made an important change in their song. Because they were flying planes into battle too, the fourth line of the first stanza was rewritten to read: "In the air, on land, and sea." Today,

the hymn is a stirring reminder to marines themselves of their own proud traditions.

With the end of the Mexican War the administra-
tion of Commandant Henderson was drawing to an
end too. There was little fighting for the marines to
do during the next ten years.

In 1857, Commandant Henderson was seventy-
four years old but he was not too old to make a final
display of the spirit he had spread through the Corps.
A political election was going on in Washington,
and one of the political parties had imported a gang
of toughs to terrorize the voters. The marines were
called out to disperse the rioters, who produced a
brass cannon, loaded and ready to fire. The marines
prepared to rush the rioters grouped behind their
gun; the crowd watching from the sidelines scamp-
ered for safety.

It was then that Commandant Henderson appeared on the scene, striding into the open, still erect,
his whiskers pure white. He walked straight to the
cannon and scornfully pushed its muzzle to the side.
A rioter fired his pistol at him and missed. Another
one was about to shoot him when one of the charging marines knocked the weapon from the rioter's

hand. The other marines quickly dispersed the gang and captured the cannon.

This was one of the final acts of Archibald Henderson, known as "the Grand Old Man of the Marine Corps." For half of his life he had been at the head of the marines. He had lived in the Commandant's house in Washington for so long that he came to regard it as his own. Forgetting that the house was actually government property, he attempted to will it to his heirs. On January 6, 1859, the brave old man died.

Confederates and Spaniards

6

THE CIVIL WAR and the reasons for which it was fought aroused loyalties that split up friends, families, states, and finally a whole nation. The Marine Corps was split by these loyalties too. As the tension mounted during the months before the outbreak, many of the Corps' most experienced officers and most of its younger ones resigned and joined the Confederacy. The government of the southern states then established a Marine Corps of its own. Thus when the struggle began, the regular Corps, like the Army and Navy, was in no condition to meet the demands that confronted the Union.

In July, 1861, the Confederate Army was forming south of Washington. The Union Army, 35,000 men under General McDowell, was poorly trained. But the people and the press cried out for action. So McDowell moved south and met the Confederates at Bull Run. With McDowell's troops was a hastily formed battalion of 348 marines, composed mainly of recruits. Some had had their weapons and equipment only a few days. Others had never carried a rifle before.

The marines were given the mission of protecting a battery of artillery. Swept by Confederate fire, they were driven back. Three times their officers rallied them. But as the battle developed during that gray afternoon, it became clear that the Federal soldiers were being out-maneuvered and out-fought. They began to fall back; the retreat became a rout; and the marines, driven from their position again, joined the retreat.

Deeply disturbed by the showing, Commandant Colonel John Harris wrote: "It was the first instance recorded in [the Corps'] history where any portion of its members turned their backs to the enemy."

The incident left the Marine Corps infinitely
wiser. The sides were clearly drawn now. There
was no longer any question of rights and wrongs. A
bitter war had to be fought, and the Corps got busy
rebuilding its organization and its pride.

During the remainder of the war, the marines
were used almost entirely as ships' detachments for
the Navy.

Marines served with the Mississippi flotilla
which, by gaining supremacy of the waterways, was
able to cut the Confederacy in two.

They fought also in the bloody assault on Fort
Fisher in December, 1864, an action which taught
them a valuable lesson.

Fort Fisher dominated the sea approach to Wil-
mington, North Carolina, the only port still open
to the Confederacy. General Ulysses S. Grant and
the Navy commanders decided to launch a large sea
and land assault against it. Fifty-six warships under
Admiral David Porter pounded the fort on Christ-
mas day, 1864. At the same time 3,000 soldiers
under General Butler moved easily along the shore
to a position close to it. But on seeing that the walls
had not been battered down by the naval gun fire,
the General decided to call off the assault. Admiral
Porter was disgusted, and his disgust seemed to have

been justified. The walls may not have been battered down, but the fort was "softened up." One of Butler's officers had even been able to climb the parapet and steal a Confederate flag, while another Union soldier had actually crept inside the fort and had come out proudly leading a horse.

Butler was replaced by General Terry, whose troops performed brilliantly when the next attack was launched on January 15, 1865. The mistake this time—far more disastrous—was made by the Navy, which decided to attack the fort on the sea side with 400 marines and 1600 sailors. The marines were to advance to positions close to the fort, and from there keep the Confederates pinned below the parapet with rifle fire. The sailors were then to advance through the marine lines and storm the parapet with pistols and cutlasses.

Neither the marines nor the sailors had been trained for such an operation which required precise timing. The sailors broke into their charge before most of the marine sharpshooters were in position so that the Confederates were not pinned down as planned. The marines were then ordered to join the frontal assault, now a mad, blind rush. Hundreds of marines and sailors were piled up dead and wounded, others dispersed in confusion.

The assault in Korea, 1871

Though the parapet was never taken, the assault was not altogether useless. The Confederates mistook it for the main Union attack, and concentrated most of their troops to oppose it. This opened the way for General Terry's men, assaulting from another direction. His force swept into Fort Fisher and after a day of fighting, captured it.

Recriminations flew back and forth for the failure of the sea-face assault. The Navy commander ashore blamed the marines for not getting into position. The Marine commander retorted that it was impossible to put them into position in the time allowed and that the sailors should have waited before beginning their charge. Neither were to blame. The operation needed weeks of planning and even rehearsal, a lesson which in years to come the Navy and marines were to put to good use.

The thirty years that followed the Civil War are known as the "Gilded Age." Business flourished, and the nation was busy harnessing the resources of the West. But life for the marines was not eventful.

There was some activity in the Far East. A detachment landed in Formosa to punish savages who had murdered shipwrecked American seamen. And for a similar reason, the marines made their first landing in Korea, then a part of the Chinese Empire.

In May, 1871, an American naval squadron anchored off the mouth of the Han River, carrying the United States minister to China, Mr. A. A. Low. His mission was to negotiate and receive assurance that outrages against shipwrecked Americans would not recur. While awaiting the arrival of the Korean officials, the naval commander, Admiral John Rodgers, sent a surveying party up the Han to study the approaches to Seoul (then Chemulpo), the Korean capital. On the way, a fort manned by at least 1,000 Korean soldiers fired at the party. The Koreans did not apologize, so Rodgers and Low decided that they should be taught a lesson.

On the morning of June 10th, 105 marines under Captain McLane Tilton, followed by 546 sailors, got into their boats and headed for the shoreline near the Korean fort. Behind them, the guns of the American ships sent shells whirring overhead and crunching into the Korean parapets. Once ashore the men moved through a bewildering tangle of hills and valleys.

The Koreans withdrew from one earthwork to another as the marines and sailors spread out

through the rice fields and woodlands. But the next
day the Koreans chose to fight in their last line of
defense, a fortress built of rock and mud.

Spaced a yard apart, the marines advanced in a
line and reached the cover of a ravine 150 yards
from the fort. Thirty yards ahead lay another ravine
where the vegetation was thick and dank. It would
offer better cover, but the field that had to be crossed
first was swept by Korean fire.

In a quick rush, Tilton and his marines gained
the ravine with the loss of only one man. From there
they could see the Koreans, strange and fearless
opponents. Wiry little men, they exposed themselves above the parapets freely, and as they fought
they chanted songs which floated over the battlefield
like some unearthly moaning. The marines poured
volleys into the figures weaving and bobbing above
the parapet.

When the sailors came abreast of the marines, the
assault began, a skillful movement as groups of marines and sailors darted forward one at a time while
others kept the Koreans pinned down with rifle fire.

The fort was systematically demolished, its guns
dumped in the river, and the thirteen dead and
wounded Americans carried back to the ship. The

marines and sailors posted guards and waited all
night for a counter-attack. None came. So the next
morning they filed back to the muddy beach and the
boats. They had had a taste of the twisted country
where later-day marines, like Lieutenant John Yancey, were to fight in one of the grimmest of wars.

The lull in marine activity that had gone on for
more than thirty years ended dramatically in 1898
with the Spanish-American War. This war lifted
the Corps from the comparative obscurity of its Civil
War and peacetime operations to a blaze of national
publicity.

On the night of February 15, 1898, the United
States battleship *Maine* lay at anchor in Havana
harbor, Cuba, a Spanish possession. Suddenly she
blew up.

The Captain's orderly, a marine private named
William Anthony, made his way below decks
through the darkness and the terrifying confusion
toward the Captain's cabin. In the passageway he
bumped into the Captain, apologized hastily and in
an exact fulfillment of his duties reported that the
ship had been blown up and was sinking. Though
hardly necessary under the circumstances, the act

was an example of marine "devotion to duty" that won the hearts of the American people. Private Anthony became a national hero.

The sinking of the *Maine* was the climax to a long period of strained relations with Spain. Though it was never definitely proved that the Spaniards caused the disaster, the feeling that they had became widespread in America, and war was declared. As usual, the marines served aboard the Navy's warships. They participated in Admiral Dewey's much celebrated victory over the Spanish fleet which he caught helpless in the confines of Manila Bay. They fired guns on Commodore Schley's cruisers and battleships when he routed Admiral Cervera's squadron. But it was an action at Guantanamo Bay, Cuba, which brought them a deluge of publicity.

On June 10, 1898, a battalion of marines under Lieutenant Colonel Robert W. Huntington landed at Guantanamo, which the Navy needed as a base for its operations. Since they were the first American troops to arrive on the Spanish island and raise the American flag, they caught the imagination of the press and were featured in the headlines for weeks. Actually, the resistance from the Spaniards was feeble. The fighting stiffened slightly when the battalion attacked the Spanish water supply at Cuzco

Well. There followed long exchanges of rifle fire across the broiling country, but the well was soon captured and Guantanamo Bay secured.

The one incident of the campaign worthy of the publicity was a sergeant's act of heroism which was prompted not by Spanish resistance but by a lack of coordination between the Navy and the marines. During the fighting for Cuzco Well, the marines signalled the warship *Dolphin* to shell the enemy positions. This she attempted to do, but she mistook the target and began dropping her shells dangerously close to the marines.

How could the bombardment be called off quickly? There were no radios to get in touch with the ships, and signal flags, merging with the foliage lining the ravines, could not be seen from the Bay. The problem was solved when a sergeant named John H. Quick stepped to the top of a ridge in no-man's land. Silhouetted against the sky, he stood in full view of the ship and of the Spanish troops as well. He was a tall man, with sloping shoulders and a serious, roughly modeled face. Enemy bullets spat around him and the *Dolphin's* shells burst close to him, but he did not seem to be aware of the danger as he wigwagged the message to stop the gunfire.

A war correspondent, Stephen Crane, described

Sergeant Quick as he waved the signal flag: "I watched his face, and it was as grave and serene as that of a man writing in his own library. I saw Quick betray only one sign of emotion. As he swung his clumsy flag to and fro, an end of it once caught on a cactus pillar. He looked annoyed!"

Lieutenant Colonel Huntington's marine battalion came home to Washington and a stirring public welcome. Behind a band blaring out "A Hot Time in the Old Town Tonight," it marched through crowds down Pennsylvania Avenue and passed in review before President McKinley. Stepping out smartly with their blue jackets, canvas leggings, and campaign hats, the marines were indeed a rousing sight.

To China and the Philippines

7

THE FIRST day of the new century was a day of
great celebration. Yet it was also a day of fearful
importance, the beginning of a half-century of wars
all over the world. For the marines, whose profession
is to fight, it began a period of activity, success, and
continued acclaim.

Until 1900 the size of the Marine Corps had
never exceeded 3000 men. But in the next sixteen
years, as it was called on to support the country's

expanding foreign policies, its strength was tripled. Previously, the marines had been armed almost entirely with rifles. Now they began to enlarge their armament with artillery, machine guns, signal gear, and airplanes. But they stressed rifle marksmanship more than ever, and their rifle teams won repeatedly in the national shooting matches.

The marines also laid greater stress on Archibald Henderson's idea of a "ready fighting force." In his day, such a force had to be gathered up from the detachments scattered through the Navy's ships and shore stations. Now, companies and battalions were formed and kept ready to go ashore as shock troops wherever they might be needed.

The first principal marine action of the century was in China. For years many countries including the United States had been trading in China where they had established business concessions. For years, also, an anti-foreign feeling had been stirring among the Chinese people. This feeling centered and grew in an organization of armed militia known as the Boxers.

In the summer of 1900 the Boxers revolted, and North China rang with their war cry, "China for the Chinese!" They murdered Chinese traders who had dealings with foreigners, seized the cities of

Peking and Tientsin, and attacked the foreign legations.

The Imperial Chinese Government did nothing
to put down the rebellion and seemed at times to
side with it. But the countries whose embassies were
besieged rushed together a joint army of 2,000 men
under an English admiral, Sir Edward Seymour.
The force, which included 112 American sailors
and marines, advanced on Peking but was driven
back by the Boxer hordes and then besieged at a
position near Tientsin. So the countries hurried in
reinforcements. The first to arrive were 450 Russian
soldiers and 137 United States Marines commanded
by Major L. W. T. "Tony" Waller.

Major Waller was a tough, impetuous, thick-set
man with a bristling mustache. His young next-in-
command, Lieutenant Smedley D. Butler, was just
as tough and impetuous, with a leathery face and a
great jutting nose. His burning gray eyes caused his
men to refer to him in later years as "Old Gimlet
Eye."

As more reinforcements arrived, Waller's marines
found themselves part of a truly international army
of 3000 men—Americans, British, Russians, Germans, Italians, and Japanese. This army, under the
command of a Japanese General named Fukushima,

moved toward the walled city of Tientsin. It relieved Admiral Seymour's besieged force and captured the foreign section of the city. Still more reinforcements arrived, including the First Marine Regiment, so that the allied strength swelled to 7500. It remained now to attack the native section of Tientsin, defended by some 50,000 Boxers.

Waller's marines were in the spearhead of Fukushima's assault that began the morning of July 13th, and Butler was in the spearhead of the marines. The path of the assault led through swamps, rice fields and rows of Chinese graves. From the wall that enclosed the native section, the Boxers laced the wet flatland with rifle and artillery fire.

As the marines drew close to the wall, Boxers began streaming from one of the gates to harass the attackers from the side. Seeing the threat, Lieutenant Butler took thirty-five men from his company and set out to drive the Chinese back into the gate. The Boxers, who could have overrun the handful of marines, stopped and watched them come at them for fifty yards. They seemed astonished by the attack, and as the determination of the marines became apparent to them, they faltered, fired a few scattered shots, and crowded back into the city, closing the huge doors behind them.

Marines were in the spearhead of the assault

Thereafter the fight did not progress easily for the Allies. The Boxer fire took many casualties, and thirty percent of Waller's marines fell, including Butler who was shot in the leg and sent to a hospital in the rear. By the end of the first day, the wall had not been breached. But the next morning a Japanese unit blew up the South Gate. The Allied troops poured through it. The Boxers, not trained or disciplined to fight hand-to-hand, put up slight resistance and fled from the city.

The next objective of this international army was Peking about 100 miles away where Allied legations were under siege. On August 4th the trek began. With Waller again marched the indefatigable Butler, now a captain, his wound still raw. The advance passed over hot, barren country where water was scarce and where the temperature rose to 140 degrees.

During the wretched march Captain Butler often wondered why he had persuaded the doctors to release him from the hospital. The pain from his leg made him weak and sick, and at times he had to cling to the saddle of a mounted officer who literally pulled him along.

On August 13th the army came in sight of ancient Peking, which was made up of four cities lying one within the other. Each was ringed by a massive wall. The outer wall enclosed the Chinese City, the second one the Tartar City, the third the Imperial City, while the innermost wall encircled the secret Forbidden City where no white man had been known to enter.

By mid-afternoon of the 13th the Allies were fighting their way to the Tartar Wall, which the Boxers had decided to defend. As Butler led his company through one of the gates he turned to shout a command and fell unconscious. Blood oozed from his chest and his men thought he had been shot through the heart. As they bent over him, they saw him stir and heard him mutter that he was all right. He pulled open his shirt. The bullet had miraculously struck the second button of his tunic. Deflected, it had gashed away some skin, taking with it part of the Marine Corps emblem tattooed on his chest. His chest turned black with the bruising, and for weeks he coughed blood. Nevertheless, that night he was back at the head of his men.

In the attack of the next day Waller's marines were used as sharpshooters. They were ordered to keep the top of the Tartar Wall clear of Boxer riflemen so that the artillery could batter it down unmolested by sniping.

Butler, his chest puffed with a bandage, discovered a channel which led to a position near the wall. It was an open sewer called the Water Gate. In a drenching night rain he led his men through the sewer muck, and under the shadow of the Tartar Wall the marines waited for the dawn. As soon as it broke, they were ready for the first Boxer head that popped up over the battlement. They fired until their rifles were white hot, while the artillery pounded holes in the wall. At noon their job was finished. The rest of the Allied forces swarmed through the breaches. As at Tientsin, the Boxers fled, and all of Peking was soon in Allied hands.

When the Boxer revolt had quieted down by autumn, 1900, Captain Butler was ordered out of China to the command of a detachment of marines aboard a warship. Typhoid fever forced him home. He recovered quickly and went on to other campaigns in other parts of the world. Major Waller remained in the East and was in action again within a year—this time in the Philippines.

The Philippine Islands had been a Spanish possession, but America had won control of them with her victory over Spain. Ever since, the United States had been busy putting down native uprisings. In late 1900 the marines, called in to help the Army, assembled in the Philippines a brigade numbering 1,678 men—the largest marine force yet grouped together.

Major Waller took command of a battalion, and in the fall of 1901, he was ordered to Samar Island. The natives of Samar, a fierce tribe called the Moros, had unexpectedly risen in revolt and had massacred a company of American soldiers, catching them unawares while they were eating breakfast. Waller's mission was to avenge the killing and crush the rebellion.

For a month Major Waller waged a harassing campaign against the Moros, leading patrols against them into the steaming jungle. Gradually, the Moros were forced to retreat inland to their last line of defenses, a series of cliffs overlooking a river named the Sohoton.

The Moros had spent three years building their cliff defenses. They had cut a whole village into the face of the cliffs towering up to 200 feet high on either side of the river. Of porous volcanic rock, the cliffs were pocked with caves which were joined by a network of trails lined with bamboo guard-rails. At points along the trails bamboo ladders sheered down to the river, and at the top of the cliff the Moros had suspended baskets filled with tons of boulders to be dropped on assailants below.

There were two approaches to the stronghold: one was the river; the other lay in the jungle behind the cliffs. Waller decided to explore both approaches. He himself took a boat detachment up the river and sent two columns into the jungle under Captains Porter and Bearss. As events developed, the river approach was never used.

Porter and Bearss discovered a Moro trail which seemed to thread upward to the rear of the cliffs. The marines moved along it carefully, noting the dangerous signs. Here was a bamboo trap or a sniper's pit. A little farther, covering a bend in the trail, were several bamboo cannon. But they saw no enemy.

The column inched along the trail to a clearing on top of one of the cliffs in the heart of the Moro stronghold. It was deserted. On the cliff across the river, however, only 150 yards away, were the Moros. They were toting rice and cutting bamboo, unaware of the force that had crept up from behind.

The marines spread out quickly. They placed an automatic gun into position, and in ten minutes they were ready, every man sighting through the thickets at the target of Moros across the river. They opened fire as one. A frightening burst in the stillness, the volley killed thirty Moros, wounded scores of others, and sent the rest fleeing into the jungle.

The marines followed up their advantage. In canoes and rafts they crossed the river and scaled the cliffs, using the bamboo ladders which the panic-stricken Moros had forgotten to destroy. Only scattered discharges of bullets and spears opposed them, and soon they had destroyed the last rallying place of the tribe.

Action in the Caribbean

8

FOR MANY years the marines remained in China and the Philippines, policing, protecting legations, garrisoning bases for the Navy. They were also sent to man outposts in the Pacific—lonely islands like Guam, Midway, and Wake which marked the American frontier in the East.

In the West other battalions and regiments of marines were waging campaigns in the hot islands and countries of the Caribbean Sea. The Caribbean at the turn of the century was a touchy area. Explosive Latin-American peoples inhabited its islands where revolts spread like brush fires. It became an American policy to intervene in the affairs of these countries and send the marines to keep order by military force.

The reason for the policy, begun by President Theodore Roosevelt, was, in most cases, briefly this: If America did not intervene, it was highly probable that certain European countries would, with the result that possible unfriendly influences might be established in the American hemisphere.

The marines fought steadily in supporting this policy from 1901 to the late twenties. It took them to five countries: Panama, Nicaragua, Haiti, Santo Domingo (The Dominican Republic), and Cuba, which became an American possession after the war with Spain. The fighting was not fierce, not to be compared to the bloody months of 1918 in France. But it was varied, filled with skirmishes, escapades, and curious episodes of marines involved in policing and even governing the Latin-Americans.

The activities of the marines in the Caribbean fill volumes by themselves. But four incidents are described here, each of which in its own particular way tells what the experience was like.

The first of the four took place in an old and weather-worn town in Santo Domingo, San Francisco de Macoris. It was November, 1916. The marines had put down one of many uprisings and had decided to establish a military government until the country could form a government of its own. But here and there remained small groups of insurgents still plotting violence. One of these was hidden in the vicinity of San Francisco de Macoris. The Governor of this place, a rebel leader named Perez, had refused to submit to military rule.

The situation was delicate indeed for the town's little marine garrison commanded by Lieutenant E. C. Williams. It would be his task to establish military rule over San Francisco de Macoris, once the official orders arrived telling him to do so. The followers of Perez might gather to oppose him in his task, but Williams faced a more threatening possibility.

There was a fort in the town. In it were jailed 100 criminals under a guard of natives whom Williams did not trust. Any moment Perez might choose to have the criminals released and armed to swell his rebel band. Williams was powerless to act without orders, but as he waited for them he made his plans.

On the evening of November 10th when the orders came to establish military rule, Perez had not yet acted. Immediately Williams sent part of his detachment to seize the police station. Then with twelve men he attacked the fort. He rushed down the main entrance toward the heavy door which was open. The Dominican guards, surprised for only an instant, opened fire. Eight marines fell wounded, but Williams and the remaining four men hurled themselves against the door as it was being closed. Pressing with all their weight, they forced it partly open.

Once inside the door Williams tried to fire his pistol but it jammed. Four feet away a Dominican raised his rifle to shoot him. In a split second a marine named Schovan jumped in front of the Lieutenant, grabbed the raised rifle by the barrel, and wrenched it from the Dominican's hands.

The fight continued briefly in the fortress hall. The Dominican guards were either killed or overpowered. The fortress, quiet now in the leaden night heat, was captured, and the criminals it housed had lost their prospect of freedom. Governor Perez, seeing that he had missed his chance of holding the town, fled into the hills where in weeks to come his band was dispersed by patroling marines.

The second episode concerns a marine sergeant named Wirkus whose first name, Faustin, caused him to be crowned a king. Wirkus was sent to Haiti where he took part in the usual patrols and skirmishes against the bandits. But, like many marines in the Caribbean campaigns, he spent much of his time policing lonely districts in the hills. Gradually he learned much about the language and customs of the natives. He found that he liked them and, in a way, pitied them. They were poverty-stricken, ignorant, and confused by the revolts that clashed around them and frightened by the columns of marines who marched through their villages.

Wirkus learned, too, how to get things done. At one of his stations, he needed a house built for himself and the native policeman whom he supervised. No money was available, so he ordered his men to round up the vagrants in the vicinity. The punishment for vagrancy in Haiti was six months of hard labor. But Wirkus sentenced the vagrants to three months and put them to work on the house. Pleased by this mild treatment, the vagrants proved enthusiastic workmen. The house was quickly built—and at no cost.

One day a Haitian woman was mistakenly brought before Wirkus as a prisoner. She was fat and wore heavy gold earrings which marked her as a figure of importance. Bowing good-naturedly, Wirkus asked her name. She was, she informed him, Ti Memenne, Queen of the island of La Gonave. Haughtily, she demanded the Sergeant's name. When he gave it—Faustin Wirkus—she looked surprised. She asked him to repeat it. Upon hearing it again she was greatly impressed and even awed. For Faustin was the name of the last King of Haiti.

The island of La Gonave had long been a source of trouble and inefficiency and it needed supervision. So Sergeant Wirkus, having made an impression on Ti Memenne, was the logical man to be sent there to be chief of police. He arrived at La Gonave tactfully bearing a present for the Queen, a five-pound box of candy wrapped in a broad silk ribbon with a big bow. The delighted Queen, who had not forgotten the white man with a king's name, gave him a party.

Wirkus made many reforms on the island of La Gonave. He built a police headquarters, using vagrants and the same system of three months' hard labor he had used before. He fired the dishonest tax collectors and installed honest men so that the island began contributing revenue to the Haitian Republic for the first time in twenty years. He built an airfield and an aqueduct to carry water to the villages from the springs in the hills. He taught the natives to plant their crops in rows, imported healthy pigs to improve the island's sickly breed, and set up a carrier-pigeon service to bring messages or vital medical supplies from the mainland.

The Queen became increasingly proud of her police chief and decided he was worthy of his name. One day she assembled her council and elected him King of La Gonave. His coronation, which went on all night, was a vivid progression of mystic rites, hollow drumbeats, and savage dancing, all of it whirling about the sergeant of Marines. A scarf was hung about his shoulders; a chicken was killed and its blood sprinkled over him. His crown, jammed uncomfortably low on his head, was a band decorated with shells, pieces of mirror, and humming bird feathers.

Though a king, Wirkus still kept up his duties as chief of police. Now, however, his 12,000 subjects held him in greater esteem than ever, and his duties multiplied. The natives brought their sick babies to him to be cured. So he requested—and got—from a puzzled supply sergeant on the mainland, a book on the care of children. Considered a judge of right and wrong, he settled family quarrels, and being a

Strafing bandits in Quilali, Nicaragua

sort of god as well, he received the people's prayers for rain when the heat was parching their crops.

So his reign went on for three years and three months. Then, in January, 1929, his detachment was ordered home and with mingled feelings of relief and regret he left the island to the farewell of the natives who lined the beach. It had been for them all a peaceful and flourishing time under King Faustin.

The next incident, dated January 1928, began along the trail to Quilali, a precipitous path that twisted into the jungle and mountains of Nicaragua. For near Quilali stood El Chipote, the stronghold of the wily Nicaraguan bandit, Sandino.

During the preceding summer Sandino's men had attacked a garrison of marines and native police at Ocotal. Now 200 marines in khaki breeches, shirts, and broad-brimmed campaign hats moved along the trail to rout out the bandit in his mountain retreat. Rounding a curve near Quilali, the head of the column was cut down by a burst of machine-gun fire. Five marines fell dead or wounded, including the commander of the column, Captain Livingston, whose arm was shattered. The marines spread out through the jungle to engage Sandino's bandits who were shooting from both sides of a ravine. Sixteen more men were wounded, but the marines gradually flushed the hidden enemy out of the ravine and pushed through to Quilali.

But at Quilali their position was hardly better. The bandits had burned part of the village and commanded the rest of it from the surrounding hills. They poured a steady fire on the marines whose plight grew steadily worse. No officers were left; there was no doctor to take care of the mounting casualties; nor was there any way to evacuate the wounded men. The report radioed to field headquarters at Ocotal was bleak.

A relief column was sent out, but it would take many days to get through. Headquarters at Ocotal was deep in gloom until a marine pilot named Lieutenant Christian Frank Schilt offered a suggestion: take the wounded out by airplane. There was no airfield at Quilali but he would drop tools to the surrounded men, so that they could cut out a strip.

Soon after, the marines at Quilali saw two biplanes roar in overhead, one of them piloted by Lieutenant Schilt. Out of them dropped crates of tools and a note which informed them of the plan. They went to work, leveling the widest road in Quilali into a strip 300 feet long and seventy feet wide. It was rough, wrinkled by ditches, and enclosed at the ends by trees and cliffs. Examining it from the air, Lieutenant Schilt decided that it would do and flew back to Ocotal to put on bigger tires to absorb the shock.

As Schilt approached for his first landing, he came in too fast and climbed away for another try. The second time he "pancaked" onto the makeshift runway. The wheels and skid slapped the ground. Bouncing over the humps and ditches, the stubby little plane jerked to a stop within 200 feet—undamaged. Marines converged around it and hauled it to the head of the strip for the takeoff. They lifted a severely wounded marine into the rear cockpit, and all the while the bandits sniped at the plane and the men.

Taking off was a more serious problem than landing. Could the plane clear the trees in 300 feet? Schilt gunned the 400-horsepower engine. The plane wobbled as it gathered speed, pounding on the roughness. Bandit rifles spattered at it. It lifted and for a second or two seemed to stay parallel to the ground. Then it began to haul itself upward, higher and higher as it neared the trees until it rose over them with a wonderful majesty.

For two days Schilt flew in and out of Quilali.

When the tail-skid snapped he kept on without it, landing on the tail itself. Struts bent under the strain, but he banged them back into shape with an axe. Altogether he made ten trips, carrying out eighteen wounded men, bringing in a new commander for the patrol and 1400 pounds of medical supplies and provisions.

Having completed this job, Schilt went on to another one. The relief column of marines, under Captain Peard, was moving up the trail to Quilali. From the air Schilt spied a bandit ambush waiting to spring on Peard's men at the same place where Captain Livingston's column had been struck. He nosed down, his machine guns blazing away at the bandits with a savagery that killed nine of them, routed the rest, and saved the patrol from falling into a trap.

The accomplishments of Lieutenant Schilt were important to the Corps not only because they saved marine lives but also because Schilt and other marine pilots flying in the Caribbean campaigns were pioneering a new science of warfare. It was a science which later came to be known as "close air support", or using planes to drop supplies, evacuate wounded, and strike at the enemy in tight cooperation with the troops on the ground. The day was to come when marine planes, directed from the front lines like barrages of artillery, were to rocket and bomb enemy positions to soften them up for the ground assault.

The last of the four Caribbean incidents took place in Haiti, 1919, and it centered on a marine sergeant named Herman Henry Hanneken. He was a silent, blond man. Tall and sinewy, he had high cheekbones, a lean jaw and pale cold eyes set in deep sockets. Few men knew what Hanneken was like as a friend. But they knew of his icy nerve and his great courage.

Hanneken was in a regiment of marines sent to Haiti when that country was swept by a revolt of the Cacos. These were Haitian bandits. They were led by a disgruntled politician named Charlemagne Peralte who strove to seize control of the country by terrorizing it. Many bandits flocked to his hideout in the mountains, and all through 1918 they burned and pillaged the villages.

Charlemagne was an elusive bandit. His hundreds of followers kept him informed of the movements of the marines so that he could maneuver his men to avoid their columns. In 1919 the marines decided to change their tactics. The commander of the regiment said simply that Charlemagne himself had to be bagged dead or alive. That would put down the uprising.

It would have to be an inside job, because Charlemagne remained far behind his troops during a battle, not even within rifle shot. Somehow, someone would have to get close to Charlemagne personally —someone with a knowledge of the language, of the country, of the people, and someone with nerve.

It was logical that Sergeant Hanneken was chosen. He had spent many months as a captain in the Haitian Gendarmerie, the native police force established and officered by the marines. He had served in the outlying stations keeping the peace, directing the civil as well as the military affairs of the Haitians. And his superiors noticed that his districts always ran without disturbance.

Sitting in his house in the town of Grande Rivière, Hanneken considered his assignment alone and in silence, as was his habit. Obviously he could not go to Charlemagne. Charlemagne must be lured to him. Hanneken thought out a plan whose complete details he would share with no one.

Soon his plan began to unfold. It started one night when a prominent citizen of Grande Rivière named Jean Conzé visited Hanneken in secret. The two men chatted long and amiably as Hanneken drew the Haitian into partnership. There was, he reminded Conzé, a reward for Charlemagne's head: $2000 in gold.

The next day the word spread through Grande Rivière that Captain Hanneken had insulted the good citizen Jean Conzé. So Conzé left Grande Rivière in a huff to join the Cacos and even made off with the Captain's beautiful pearl-handled pistol. Another Haitian also left town that day to join the Cacos. He was Jean Edouard François, one of Hanneken's gendarmes who, it was said, had been mistreated by the Captain.

François, whose handwriting was fine and legible, became Charlemagne's private secretary. Conzé became a bandit leader, well equipped with arms, food and rum secretly provided by Hanneken. He grew bold and sent letters into Grande Rivière attacking the character of the Captain of Gendarmes. He plundered a village and captured some women. Grande Rivière was soon buzzing over his activities. Word too began to filter to Charlemagne.

Conzé's prowess rose to truly astonishing heights. He built a fort named Capois and dared Hanneken to attack it. This Hanneken did one night, and before the battle had hardly begun he ordered his astonished trumpeter to blow retreat. He even reeled behind a bush as though shot and when no one was looking he smeared red ink on his arm and bound it with a bandage. He walked around the streets of Grande Rivière with his arm in a sling, his head bent, taking the gibes of the villagers and the silent, puzzled looks of other marines who knew nothing of what was really going on.

The people of Grand Rivière were stunned by the victory they thought was real. This Captain of Gendarmes was indeed an easy mark for the brave Cacos of Conzé! Conzé, meanwhile, was now in close touch with Charlemagne, writing fiery letters. Wouldn't Charlemagne come down from the mountains to lead an all-out attack on Grande Rivière? His troops and leadership were needed. And this Hanneken, after all, was no match for the Cacos as he, Jean Conzé, had proved at Capois!

One night in October Conzé slipped into Grande Rivière with the news for which Hanneken had waited and planned. Charlemagne had agreed to come out of the hills. He would attack Grand Rivière on the last night of the month, and on the way to the fight he would pass through a village called Mazaire where Hanneken could lie in wait.

After dark on October 31st, Hanneken and a

marine corporal named William Button blackened themselves with burned cork and put on the rags of a Caco. Then with ten disguised gendarmes, they stole through the marine lines awaiting the attack and went on to Mazaire. Hiding in the bushes, they watched more than 700 Cacos file down the trail. In the shadows they were met suddenly by Jean Edouard François, who bore disturbing news. Charlemagne, he said between breaths, had decided not to come through Mazaire and was camped back on a hill, waiting for reports of the battle.

Hanneken took the news in silence, but he was thinking hard. He could hear rifles crackling—the attack on Grande Rivière was already beginning. For four months he had worked to trap the bandit leader. There was only one thing left to do. He told François to guide him to Charlemagne's camp, and he set off through the Caco lines as fast as his long strides could carry him, followed by Button and the gendarmes. Fortunately, the night lay dense under heavy banks of clouds.

At midnight they reached the first of five outposts protecting Charlemagne's camp. François gave the password, "General Jean" (in honor of Conzé) and said they were messengers bringing Charlemagne news of a great victory at Grande Rivière. They were sent through with happy Caco shouts ringing out behind them. Three more outposts let them by without question. But the last was Charlemagne's personal bodyguard, grouped around the foot of a knoll on top of which glowed the light of a campfire.

"He is up there, *mon capitaine*," whispered François, who faded away into the darkness so as not to be recognized by the guards who knew him.

The figure of a huge Negro with a raised pistol blocked the trail to the knoll. Hanneken muttered the password and pushed on by him. But the Negro held Button by the arm, asking him where he had found such a fine automatic rifle. Button improvised a Caco mumble and brushed on.

By the campfire Charlemagne sat with his women. He was a squat, brown man. On his belt he wore Hanneken's pearl-handled pistol, given to him by Cónzé, and a silk shirt that gleamed in the light. Hanneken strode directly to the fire, and with a different pistol took aim and shot a bullet through the silk shirt into Charlemagne's chest. At the same moment Button sprayed the guards below with his automatic rifle.

Panic gripped the bewildered Cacos clumped around the knoll. A woman threw a blanket over the fire and smothered it. In the darkness Hanneken ducked and groped his way through the hubbub of wild shots and shouts to Charlemagne, who he saw was dead. He dragged the body behind some rocks and lay there near it, hugging the ground as bullets snapped in every direction.

When daylight came Hanneken and his party were alone and unhurt. The Cacos had taken to the bush. Hanneken threw Charlemagne's body on a stray pony and took it down to Grande Rivière where the gaping villagers lined the streets to see it. Then it was taken to Cap Haitien where it lay in a public place so that more people could be assured that the Caco chief was truly dead. The Cacos spluttered back feebly, but by 1920 their rebellion was as dead as Charlemagne, and the countryside was peaceful once again.

"Pas Fini"

9

IN THE summer of 1916 while the Caribbean campaigns were in progress, the First World War was in its third year. At home, the marines were preparing for a possibility that seemed likely to come true: America might join the fighting in France. Congress passed the National Defense Act, which authorized greater strength for the Army, Navy, and Marine Corps. Then, on April 6, 1917, Congress declared war on Germany.

The Marine Commandant, Major General George Barnett, proposed that the marines should serve both the Navy and the Army as they had many times in their history. President Wilson agreed.

After the declaration of war the Corps was deluged by many more recruits than it could accept—lawyers, teachers, business men, and thousands of college students. Three hundred students from the University of Minnesota, for example, enlisted in one bloc.

Regiments and brigades were formed to fill the Corps' multiple duties—an advance base force to strengthen the Caribbean area where many marines were already committed; a brigade in Texas to defend the oil fields against possible attack from Mexico; detachments aboard the Navy's warships; and two brigades, the 4th and the 5th, to be sent to France.

The 5th Brigade in France was split up into small units to guard supply depots, docks, and camps. It never saw action, and the men felt bitter and humiliated as they saw regiment after regiment of Americans march to the front. But the 4th Brigade, consisting of the 5th and 6th Regiments and a machine gun battalion, fought in the spearhead of the American armies.

The 4th arrived in France during the spring and summer of 1917. The war the marines were about to enter had become a science of its own, learned by the Allies at brutal cost. The marines were placed under the instruction of some of the finest French troops, including the Alpine Chasseurs, the "blue devils" of France. The training was unrelenting— weeks of sham trench warfare, daily hikes of sixteen to twenty-six miles, forced marches, patrols, raids, gas attacks, and practice in relieving other troops at night. The men became lean and tough.

Winter, 1918, blew in with storms that changed the country roads to streams of mud. The training and the hiking went on and by March the Brigade was ready to go to the front. It was formed as part of the Army's Second Division, under General Omar Bundy, with the remainder consisting of artillery and the 9th and 23rd Regiments.

The men were sent to a quiet sector near the city of Toulon where experience came slowly but surely. They learned to patrol at night, ducking from one shell hole to another or wriggling under the barbed wire to locate the enemy positions and discover his strength.

There were sudden German raids, repelled successfully by marines proud to have bagged their first enemy soldier. There were occasional artillery barrages, the German shells screaming desperately close or crashing into the trenches to shatter the bodies of a few marines crouched against the side. There was mud thick to the knees, lice, rats, and eternal dampness.

The Brigade commander, Colonel Charles A. Doyen, fell sick and was sent home. Since no marine officer was available in France to take command, General Pershing, commander of the American armies in France, gave the Brigade to Brigadier General James G. Harbord of the Army. Harbord was a hard-driving but tactful officer, fully conscious of marine pride. He won the affection of the marines right away by telling them that Pershing, on giving him command of them, had said, "You are to have charge of the finest body of troops in France, and if they fail to live up to that reputation, I shall know whom to blame."

While the marines were in the trenches near Toulon, the Germans launched a huge offensive in the northwest. It drove through the juncture of the French and British lines, rolling steadily toward Amiens and across the Somme River.

In early May, the 2nd Division was moved from the Toulon sector to a reserve position near Paris.

The German offensive, meanwhile, veered south, gathering strength. The French, battered by three years of brutal fighting and staggering casualties, were hurled back before it. By May 30th, the Germans had penetrated to the village of Château-Thierry on the Marne River. Paris lay only fifty miles ahead.

The Marne was a rallying cry for the French. At Château-Thierry they held firm as they had in 1914, and they were helped by American soldiers. So the Germans shifted their attack, probed northwest of the town and found a weak spot. They punched down the Metz-Paris road, and in that sector the weary French collapsed.

The French command did not believe that the 2nd Division had had enough experience to be sent into a pitched battle. Even so, the threat to Paris was so acute that Marshal Foch decided to rush the Americans into the gap on the Metz-Paris road. The call came to the 4th Brigade on the evening of May 30th. That night it waited to be taken to the front in camions, French trucks with seats on the sides hooded by canvas covers like prairie schooners. With the dawn, the camions arrived. The marines packed into them and rattled off into the morning.

Not until the next noon was the Brigade assembled together at Montreuil-aux-Lions behind the front. That afternoon, as the marines moved up to the line, they passed columns of retreating Frenchmen, their bruised and soiled faces covered with despair. To these French soldiers, who had fought for countless months, the war seemed over and lost. *"La guerre est finie"*—"the war is ended"—they said over and over again on the road. Just as many times the marines walking past mustered their slim store of the French language to retort, *"pas fini"*—"it's not ended." They said it so much that that area came to be known officially as the *"Pas Fini"* sector.

The marines went on past the columns of sagging Frenchmen. They took up positions along a line that wound through the edges of woods and over gently rolling farmland. In front of them French units had been formed in a ragged line.

On June 2nd the marines awoke to brace themselves for the attack that was expected that day. At 5 P.M. it emerged from the woods in front of a battalion of the 5th Marines. Waves of Germans in gray with the sun gleaming on their helmets moved across an open slope where wheat and poppies mingled their bright colors. The enemy came in two columns, a fine spectacle of military precision. It struck the French line which buckled.

As the French soldiers retreated, the Germans came on confidently behind them. They did not know that a battalion of marines lay along the crest of the next hill with its rifles and machine guns trained on them.

When the French had passed through the marine lines, a gale of metal swept into the Boche (German) ranks, and behind it went months of careful training in marksmanship that was deadly in its effect. Scores of Germans toppled over among the wheat and the poppies. The attack hesitated and broke. It came back again, reformed, but again it cracked under the fire from a surprising enemy that suddenly seemed to have taken heart. A third time it tried, and as the slaughter mounted, the Germans gave up the attack and ran back into the woods. There, shells from American artillery crashed into them and caught them above ground. A French plane observing overhead waggled "Bravo!"

The stand on the Metz-Paris Road and the French-American victory at the village of Château-Thierry blunted the German offensive in that area. But the salient still prodded like a huge fang into the Allied lines defending Paris. The French commander ordered the Americans to join in a series of

Allied offensives that would straighten the line and strike the enemy while he was still reeling from the two defeats.

It fell to the 4th Marine Brigade to attack Belleau Wood and the village of Bouresches that lay on a road junction east of it. The Wood was a dense forest of thin, tall trees. It stood on high rocky ground, and in the hands of the Germans it threatened the flank of Château-Thierry which had to be held at all cost. From it the Germans could launch attacks that could disrupt the entire Allied line in the south.

Before the marines lay a field of wheat from 200 to 600 yards wide. On the other side of it Belleau Wood rose like a black, ominous scowl on the landscape. It was not known how many Germans were inside of it. The French guessed that there were relatively few, but the Americans had spotted considerable numbers of the enemy. As it turned out, the attack of the 4th Brigade, scheduled for 5 P.M. June 6th, was launched against a total of two German divisions.

At 4:30 P.M. the artillery began. It was a routine barrage—a longer one would have warned the Germans that a full-scale attack was about to start. Zero hour seemed maddeningly slow in coming. But

Belleau Wood, 1918

when it came a single shout echoed along the trench, and the marines went over the top into the wheat.

The entire side of the forest burst into a raving of German machine guns and rifles. The marines did not charge through the storm of bullets. They walked, so that they would not be out of breath when they reached the woods and closed with the Boches. They were formed in lines twenty yards apart with five-yard intervals between men. Great rents were torn in the lines, but the formation kept walking, pausing, shooting, and walking again. There was no shouting. The men muttered, complained, and cursed but kept walking. And as they walked, the wheat bowed and waved over the hundreds who fell in it.

One battalion commanded by Major Berry was almost wiped out before it reached the woods. The other under Major Sibley was more fortunate because it had less distance to walk. When it drew near to the forest it broke into the charge. The men of the battalion had spotted gray shapes in the shadows, heaving grenades or crouched behind the spitting muzzles of machine guns.

Germans swarmed in the forest. Machine guns were everywhere—in ravines, in the tree tops, behind heaps of rocks and piles of cut timber. Had the marines hesitated they would have been destroyed to a man. But their assault gathered speed, fury and a spirit of revenge for the dead lying in the wheat. They ran through the crossfire and assaulted the individual machine gun nests that were delivering it. They broke into small groups which fought like Indians. Darting from tree to tree and rock to rock, they worked to the rear or flanks of the Boche nests.

The Germans fought bitterly, using every wile they knew. A Boche would throw up his hands, yelling "Kamerad." Behind him other Germans crawled unseen, using him to lure the Americans into the open. At first the tricks worked. But soon the marines gave no quarter.

By 10 o'clock the battle had quieted down and the remnants of Sibley's battalion held a foothold in the southwestern corner of Belleau Woods. Fighting flared up now and then during the night, but reinforcements streamed in to dig trenches and to strengthen the position.

Meanwhile, to the east of the Wood, another assault had been made shortly after Sibley's and Berry's men had set out across the wheat field. A company moved toward the town of Bouresches. These marines advanced as the others had. There were not many left when they reached Bouresches where 300 to 400 Germans waited for them. Captain Duncan, who walked along with a pipe in his mouth, was shot down. So Lieutenant Robertson led the assault on the town.

The Germans defended from the street corners and the housetops. One by one, their gun nests were grenaded and bayoneted, but one by one the marines fell until only Lieutenant Robertson and twenty men were left.

At 9:45 reinforcements arrived and soon after, part of the town was in marine hands. But ammunition had run low and the Germans were preparing to counterattack. When this news came to headquarters, a lieutenant named William Moore and a sergeant major named Quick (hero of Guantanamo Bay) volunteered to take a truck load of ammunition through the German fire to Bouresches. The truck swayed over the gutted road, swerving crazily through falling artillery shells. It drove straight into the fire of the Boche machine guns, but still it kept going and rumbled into Bouresches untouched.

The ammunition saved the marines in Bouresches. By June 8th the town was secure and the marine line was extended west to join Sibley's battalion in Belleau Wood.

The battle for the forest was by no means over. It went on for eighteen more days, as company after company of marines was pitted into the teeth of the German front. Barrages of gas forced them to don the breathless masks, and there was no respite from the ugly, bitter in-fighting. But the assault carried through the forest which was now a splintered shambles. When the marines emerged into the open fields and the clear light of day, 4000 of them had fallen, almost sixty per cent of the Brigade. But they had wrenched a valuable piece of ground from the Germans and had killed or captured 3000 of them.

The French paid a tribute to the marines. They renamed the forest Bois de la Brigade de Marine, and they gave the Brigade a citation as well. The marines also received attention from the enemy. The Germans had been contemptuous of the supposedly inexperienced American troops. But they placed the 2nd Division in their highest classification of battle efficiency, "a shock unit." They were singularly impressed by the Americans who wore a globe and anchor on their uniforms. An intelligence report to General von Ludendorff referred to them as *Teufel Hunden*—Devil Dogs.

The Allied armies in Europe pressed ahead, both in the north and south of the entire line. The 2nd Division was committed to battle four more times in the offensives that sent the Germans reeling and ended with the Armistice on November 11, 1918. The 4th Brigade was in the thick of them.

The first was at Soissons. In a quick massing of troops, Marshal Foch concentrated a large force at a German weak spot. In the haste of the preparations, the marines did not have time to bring up all their machine guns before zero hour.

"Very well," said an officer of the 6th Regiment on hearing this news, "we'll take the Boche machine guns."

The attack tore through woods and across another wheat field where battalions of the 6th assaulted through an artillery barrage that took 1300 casualties. As at Belleau Wood, they kept on. The 2nd Division, with the 1st American and French Moroccan Divisions, was given the credit for spearheading the attack that began the general retreat of the German Army in that area.

After Soissons, the 2nd Division was placed under the command of a marine, Major General John A. Lejeune. He led it during the next American attack aimed at flattening the German salient that ex-

tended to the village of St. Mihiel. The offensive
caught the Germans just as they themselves were
about to withdraw. The victory was won with com-
paratively few casualties.

In the Argonne Sector the 2nd Division drew the
assignment of capturing Blanc Mont, a fortified hill
pocked with guns and rimmed by trench networks.
The marines and soldiers jumped off on October 3,
1918. For some of the marine battalions it was as
bloody as Belleau Wood. In another series of sustained, leaping dashes, the bewildered Germans
were overrun and the hill taken in three days. The
French were astonished by the speed and success of
the attack. To both the 5th and the 6th Marine Regiments they awarded the "fourragère." The 5th and
6th Marines still wear this decoration which is now
part of their regimental uniform—a woven green
and red cord that hangs over the left shoulder.

The 2nd Division was put into the line again to
take part in the final drive to the Meuse River that
began November 1st. The armed might of France
and America jumped off that day. The Marine Brigade led the attack of the 2nd Division near the
center of the Allied line. The planning was thor-
ough; the artillery support long and devastating. For
the next ten days the tide poured on, and before it

the Germans could only fall back across the Meuse River where they hoped to make a stand.

In one sector, on the night of the 10th, the commanders of assaulting marine battalions conferred together near the river bank. Should they make a crossing that night? It was true that the orders to cross had come through at 5 P.M. But in the haste of the offensive, confusion had set in everywhere. The hour for the crossing was vague. The Allied artillery preparation had begun and ended too soon. The engineers had not been able to lay the pontoon bridges across the river because the Boche artillery fire had stiffened. So the battalion commanders agreed to put off the attack until morning. They were glad they did. The word came soon after that the Armistice had been signed, and at 11 A.M. the fighting would end.

Guadalcanal, Tarawa and Iwo Jima
10

DURING THE years between the two World Wars, the marines were confronted by a problem. Their mission as sea-soldiers had become complicated by advances in weapons and fighting techniques. In the old days it had been simple to load marines into longboats and row them to the beach. Now, tanks, big guns, bulldozers, trucks, quantities of fuel and ammunition had to be landed along with the men. Also, greater numbers of troops had to be put ashore at once to mass the power to destroy beach defenses built and armed on the latest principles.

So the marines evolved and wrote down the science of amphibious warfare—the modern attack against a modern beach defense. To put the new science into effect, they established the Fleet Marine Force, the new "ready" fighting arm of the Corps.

Working closely with the Navy, the marines rehearsed and perfected their amphibious technique. They scrambled down cargo nets hung over the sides of transport ships. They took their places in powered landing boats which formed into waves (or lines) and headed shoreward at planned intervals.

Ashore the marines learned to jump from boats quickly and to fan out across the beach in the running assault. With the attack, they coordinated the support of gunfire and of planes flying from the Navy's carriers.

The "shore party" was developed—marines who stacked supplies on the beach and channeled them inland. To carry the supplies, they used a machine called the "alligator." Built of steel with a tracked chain clanking around and around on either side, it could move over solid land or plow through sea and swamp.

When World War II came, the work of the marines during peace time proved immensely valuable. To a great extent, World War II was to be an amphibious war. Landings would be made in Africa, Sicily, Italy and France, and on Pacific islands that were held by the Japanese. Most of the landings would be made by the Army, which had been unable to concentrate on the amphibious specialty. So the marines taught the Army what they had learned.

On December 7, 1941, Japanese bombers sneaked in over Pearl Harbor and opened their war against the United States. American planes and warships sitting idly on the airfields and in the harbor went up in an inferno. The Japanese offensive struck all along the Pacific frontier where small detachments of marines garrisoning the islands put up brave but useless resistance. Guam was overrun. Wake Island fell after a sixteen-day defense which beat off one attack and forced the Japanese to reform their forces and land in strength.

In the Philippines a greater catastrophe was in the making—the worst defeat America ever suffered. Outnumbered, their communications shattered, the Americans on Bataan surrendered to the Japanese. Other United States troops under General Jonathan Wainwright, made the last stand on Corregidor, a sun-blistered rock in the middle of Manila Bay. The island was a helpless target for the Japanese warships in the harbor and the Japanese artillery on Bataan peninsula. The 4th Marine Regiment, manning the beach defenses, saw its guns blown to pieces or buried under landslides as the Japanese shells exploded in the soil. The bombardment of Corregidor thundered on for one terrible month. Then, on the night of May 5, 1942, the Japanese landed, and the next day General Wainwright's dazed troops had no choice but to surrender.

The war which the United States waged against the Japanese was vast and complicated—one which the Japanese had believed impossible. It began with the Navy's first attempt to win control of the sea. In May and June of 1942, the Navy fought and defeated the Japanese fleet twice. These victories turned the tide by relieving the threat against American sea lanes. As a result, the way was opened for the United States to attack the strongholds which the Japanese were building on the Pacific islands.

America attacked with ships, planes, marines and amphibiously-trained soldiers. The first strikes began on a small scale on the outer fringe of the new

Japanese Empire. Amphibious troops landed and seized islands with airfields and harbors. From these, American planes and ships could strike still deeper into the Empire.

As the war went on, more landings were made, leapfrogging deeper into the islands which led like stepping stones to Japan itself.

The offensive was divided into two main thrusts. One, in the Southwest Pacific, was under the command of General Douglas MacArthur. It leapfrogged up the coast of New Guinea to the Philippines. The other, under Admiral Chester Nimitz, island-hopped across the Central Pacific. The two thrusts finally converged on the island of Okinawa, a few hundred miles south of Japan. Okinawa was cleared of the enemy and the combined might of America prepared to attack Japan itself. The invasion was never made. The atomic bomb, dropped on Hiroshima and Nagasaki, persuaded the Japanese to surrender.

In both the Southwest and Central Pacific the marines took part in some of the hottest fighting in all history. To fill its missions the Corps multiplied its strength from 19,400 men in 1940 to 485,052 by the time the war ended. It built its striking arm, the Fleet Marine Force, from one brigade to six full divisions. With these, it fought in twenty major campaigns.

The cost was high — 19,670 dead, 67,134 wounded—but the places taken were of major importance in winning the war. There is not room here to describe the actions that occurred in all of them. But there are three—each a memorable name—which tell the story of how the marines fought in the Pacific.

Guadalcanal

Guadalcanal lay near the foot of a chain of islands called the Solomons. It had been a peaceful place, in the backwash of Pacific trade, where Australian coconut planters had quietly gone about their business in the cooler hours of the broiling days. In the spring of 1942 the Japanese landed on Guadalcanal.

Australian planters hid in the jungle and observed the enemy through a secret system of "coast watchers." In this way they were able to report that the Japanese were hard at work building an airfield on the island. This was threatening news, and it convinced the American command that Guadalcanal had to be seized immediately.

With the dawn of August 7, 1942, a column of cruisers, destroyers and troop transports slipped around the western tip of Guadalcanal. Along the coast behind the whitening beach line stood row after row of palm trees. Behind them lay the wet gray jungle, with ridges rising above it like giant fishbacks that gradually bulged away into mountains. These cut the 80-mile length of the island in two.

As the sun threw its bands across the dull sky, orange flame lashed out from the guns of the warships. Carrier planes dived toward the beach, their machine guns crackling as they sprayed the coconut groves. The beaches erupted in clouds of sand, and the sounds boomed across the still channel.

Aboard the transports the men of the First Marine Division, commanded by Major General A. A. Vandegrift, waited below the hot decks. Loudspeakers scattered throughout the ships blared out a command: "Now all marines go to your debarkation stations."

The troops filed up narrow ladders to positions on deck above the cargo nets that were draped over the sides. More orders crackled in the speakers. Davits were swung out and landing craft lowered. Marines swarmed down the nets into the boats which, one by one, scooted off to "rendezvous" areas where they waited, circling. Wave following wave, the boats sped for the beach. The first United States offensive of World War II had begun.

The marines did not throw all of their force on Guadalcanal. They also sent units to seize Tulagi and Florida Islands on the other side of Sealark Channel. At Tulagi they met brief resistance. But on Guadalcanal the Japanese, mostly laborers, fled into the hills. The marines of the assault waves secured the beachhead without firing a shot. Those landing behind them rushed across the beach with a sense of history-in-the-making only to find their comrades sitting in the grass unconcerned, hacking open coconuts with their bayonets.

The advance to the airfield was also unopposed. But after pushing inland some of the battalions found themselves in land uncharted on their maps. Platoons and companies got lost. They sweated, cursed and trudged over jagged ridges, through wet meshes of jungle and knifelike Kunai grass as tall as a man. They were bogged down in swamps, bitten by scorpions and beaten by the suffocating heat. Had the enemy been prepared for the attack they could have destroyed the marines piecemeal as they wandered about wondering where they were.

By the end of the second day the confusion began to straighten itself out. The airfield was captured, and one by one the units straggled in from the jungle and Kunai grass to form an organized perimeter around it.

The Japanese, meanwhile, had begun to fight back. Planes flying in from bases to the northeast attacked the American convoy and set fire to one transport. Japanese warships were also approaching. On the night of August 9th, they slipped unnoticed into the middle of the American warships. They fired salvo after salvo, and for thirteen minutes the channel lit up with flashes and echoed with explosions. The silence that followed lasted until dawn, when the Japanese ships slipped away as suddenly as they had come. Behind them they left one Australian and four American cruisers sunk or severely damaged.

The next morning the Navy weighed anchor, limped out of the channel and disappeared to the south. It had planned to leave even before the Japanese attack began, as fuel for its carrier planes had run low. But the defeat probably hastened its departure.

Around the thin perimeter, the marines prepared themselves for whatever was to come. In places they had to leave huge gaps in the line because there were not enough men to keep it solid. Nor was there enough food. The abrupt departure of the Navy had left little behind for the marines. However, they found stores of rice and canned fish in the captured thatched shacks on the airfield. These were cooked up into a variety of impromptu dishes, to go occasionally with a rare can of American beans, hash or Vienna sausage.

There was, too, a herd of cattle wandering around the fields which had been owned by the planters inhabiting the island. These animals were eyed hungrily by the marines, who sneaked off every so often to bring back to their platoon slabs of lean steak. Before long the medical corps put a stop to this, declaring the cattle to be tubercular. One dark night, the cattle wandered between two units of marines which, thinking the animals were the enemy, opened up on each other in a whizzing burst of fire. It ended only when the startled animals were heard to clump off in a panic.

Many shovels, axes, ponchos, tents, water cans, and much medical equipment were also still lying in the holds of the Navy's transports somewhere at sea. The scarcity of mosquito nets was a serious matter for hordes of mosquitoes feasted on the unprotected men. Next to the Japanese in days to come, malaria was to be the marines' worst enemy. Emplacements were dug with the small inadequate entrenching tools marines carried on their backs. Coconut logs were chopped down with machetes or a precious axe passed along the line from one platoon to another. Fire lanes for the machine guns had to be cleared through the jungle with bayonets when the over-worked machetes snapped in two.

Work on the airfield went ahead with as much speed as the lack of tools would permit. The field was needed desperately to help defend the perimeter. Night after night, ominous sounds of cruising Japanese ships came from the harbor. They were steaming to the east where they were landing troops. On August 18th a patrol of marines ambushed and wiped out a party of Japanese heading to scout out the perimeter.

The airfield was ready now. But where were the planes? The first flight of them flew in from a carrier on August 20th—stubby, sturdy Hellcats with white stars on their wings.

They came not a moment too soon. The next morning, in the early hours of August 21st, the Japanese struck. Nine hundred of them hurled themselves across a sandspit at the mouth of the Tenaru river. The handful of marines at that point held fast behind their makeshift emplacements, pouring bullets and shells into the on-rushing Japanese.

The dawn that came slowly revealed ghastly heaps of torn Japanese bodies on the sandspit. On the other side of the river, Japanese troops had dug in and were firing. The Hellcats, on their first mission, roared in and strafed them.

A marine battalion crossed the river and pushed down the opposite bank. It assaulted the Japanese on the flank and drove them like rabbits into the sea. The Japanese commander, his confidence badly shaken, burned his regimental flag and shot himself through the head.

The marines settled down to await the next attack. The Hellcats went up to meet the enemy Zeros in whirling dogfights. Always outnumbered in those early days, the marine aviators accomplished amazing feats of piloting and shot down scores of enemy planes. But they could not defy the law of averages forever. One by one almost all of the original squadron were shot down.

At nights the Japanese did their best to harass the marines out of their sleep. They would send over one lone plane which would drop bombs at random. The

marines learned to ignore it, contemptuously dub-
bing it "Washing Machine Charlie" or "Louie the
Louse." But many times enemy warships, unopposed
in the defenseless harbor, bombarded the perimeter.
Their shells would plow into the revetments with
fearful explosions, forcing the marines to dive for
their deepest foxholes. In the morning, there would
be scenes of destruction to clear away, including the
bodies of men whose "number was up."

The second Japanese attack was many times
stronger than the first, and it was elaborately
planned. It consisted of three prongs that were supposed to strike the marine line simultaneously at
three different places. But the Japanese fell victim
to the jungle. Their columns bogged down, lost com-
munication with each other and struck the marines
separately. Two of the enemy columns, exhausted
by the trek through the jungle, were easily wiped
out. The main assault, however, came close to pushing through to the airfield.

It began the night of September 12th in the eerie
blackness of the jungle.

It struck at a vulnerable point where the line had
not been built up. In fact, the units there were actually supposed to be resting. Soon the marines found

themselves tussling with Japanese in the dark with knives, bayonets and fists. Platoons and companies were cut off as Japs infiltrated through the lines, but they managed to free themselves, pulling back to a ridge where they could fight in the open. There the Japanese spread a smoke screen and cried out "Gas!" They tried other tricks, cursing, joking and shouting faked commands in queer, high-pitched English. At one point, only sixty marines were left to defend the ridge.

The marine artillery went into action, hurling the biggest barrage of the campaign. Two thousand shells crashed on the ridge slopes and the jungle barely 200 yards in front of the marines. For two nights and a day the battle flared off and on, and when the third morning came, the Japanese had thrown their last against the ridge. Fifteen hundred of them lay dead in the jungle and on the slopes of the ridge that came to be known in history as "Bloody Ridge."

The Japanese desperately wanted Guadalcanal which was of high strategic value. It came as a shock to them that the flower of their army could not defeat the Americans. The marines on the island chuckled when they heard that the propagandist in Tokyo referred to them as the "Butchers of Guadalcanal."

Iwo Jima, 1945

Actually, the butchers were the Japanese who insisted on butchering themselves.

The Japanese prepared for another offensive. But the marines were readier than they had ever been since August 7th. The Navy had returned to Guadalcanal, bringing barbed wire, tools, food and even shaving lotion. Army planes had joined marine squadrons on the airfield. A regiment of marines arrived followed later by an Army regiment. With this new strength the gaps in the line were filled and the perimeter expanded.

The third Japanese attack came in late October. It was preceded by a massive naval bombardment which damaged almost all the American planes on the airstrip. Torrents of rain caved in the runways, and turned the vital roads joining the marine positions into quagmires. The situation was serious indeed when the attack struck the marine lines.

Fortunately, Japanese planning broke down once again. The assaults struck separately and were destroyed separately. In one sector, during two nights of fighting, the Japanese stormed the fortified marine line seven times with amazing disregard for their own lives. In the Japanese code it was an honor to die for the Emperor and a disgrace to be captured. In all, 3400 of them were thus honored.

The lieutenant colonel commanding the unit that bore the brunt of the assault was hit by seven shell fragments. The medical corpsman took one look at him and began writing out the usual tag which is attached to the wounded so that they are promptly evacuated to the field hospitals.

"Take that d— label and paste it on a bottle!" roared the outraged Colonel, his chin protruding farther than usual. "I remain in command here!" He did, too.

Still the Japanese did not give up. In November they amassed at Rabaul, their stronghold northeast of Guadalcanal, a huge invasion force which they packed into twelve transports. Protected by a fleet of warships, these sallied forth to Guadalcanal. Meanwhile, news of the approaching task force reached the United States, which was anxiously watching the progress of the marines. Hysterical news commentators gave the marines slim chance to survive the attack. The Navy, they said, had decided to abandon the leathernecks to their doom rather than risk more ships.

Nothing could have been further from the truth. The Navy steamed into the Japanese fleet and in two brilliant night battles routed it. The Japanese transports tried to make a run for the Guadalcanal shore. American planes swarming up from the airfield sank or set fire to eight of them. The remaining four transports reached the beach, but before they could unload, long-range artillery and more planes had reduced them to flaming hulks. They can be seen there today, charred, half-sunken remnants of the last major attempt of the Japanese to retake the precious island.

As November drew to an end, Army regiments came in to take over and expand the perimeter further. The marines, who had lost 4,272 dead and wounded, were removed from the island they had made famous. They were wracked with malaria, dysentery and covered with the spreading sores of "jungle rot." Their faces had a yellow pallor. Their bodies were permeated with the dampness and sour smell of the jungle. Some of them were so weak that they could not make the long climb to the decks of the transports. They had learned many lessons about amphibious warfare, weapons, jungle fighting and about their tricky, tenacious and foolish enemy.

Tarawa

By the autumn of 1943 the Solomon Island chain was under American control, and General Mac-

Arthur's divisions were leapfrogging up the coast of New Guinea. So it was decided to begin the thrust through the Central Pacific. The first blow was aimed at the islands of the Tarawa Atoll. One of these was Betio Island which, on November 20, 1943, was assaulted by the 2nd Marine Division.

Betio was a tiny, low lump of coral where the only vegetation was the inevitable palm tree. Around the island lay a natural fortification—a vast and treacherous reef. Worse, the tides that swirled over the reef were hard to predict. Called "dodging tides," they varied so much that no one could tell whether the water at a certain time would be deep enough to float the landing boats.

On the island itself, the Japanese had crammed 4,836 troops who were entrenched in giant pillboxes of rock, steel and concrete and in countless cleverly hidden holes. The Japanese commander declared that a million men, fighting for a hundred years, could not assault and seize Betio.

The American Admiral, in command of the ships which would bombard the island before the landing, was equally confident. He said to marine officers: "We do not intend to neutralize this island; we do not intend to destroy it. Gentlemen, we will obliterate it!"

On D-day the sky above Betio was brown with flying sand, smoke and flaming coconut trees. To get over the reef, the first waves of marines were placed in "alligators"—the first time these machines were used to carry assault troops. They crawled toward the beach as the naval shells screamed above them. They came to the reef where the water was shallower than expected. Despite this the "alligators" ground over the reef, pitching and tilting on the rough coral.

The marines in the following waves were loaded in landing boats because there were not enough "alligators" to carry them too. The boats came on toward the beach, but within 400 to 800 yards of it they struck the reef. They could go no further. The marines jumped into the pale green water and, holding their rifles above their heads, began to wade.

From the beach came a sudden clatter of fire— machine guns, mortars and the awful thumping of bigger guns. The bullets and explosives rained into the wading figures with their weapons held high. The water kicked up viciously in speckles of foam or burst into tall spouts.

Marines were shot helpless in the water. They stepped into holes in the reef and, unable to shake off the heavy equipment on their backs, drowned.

Boatloads of men struck by the bigger shells literally disintegrated. The "alligators" churning back from the beach tried to take on the boatloads before they were hit. But some of the alligators broke down. Others, burst into fiery cauldrons.

The marines kept walking— as they had across the wheat field at Belleau Wood. They died horribly in the water now bobbing with hundreds of American dead. They died on the barbed wire strung in front of the beach, or in the gentle surf licking along the sand. Some of them survived the gauntlet only to die inches from the Japanese guns that were committing the slaughter. The marines who got through alive were helpless and furious as they saw their friends mowed down.

That night there was only a thin marine foothold on the ghastly beach. No artillery had gotten ashore. It didn't matter—there was no room to set it up. Naval gunfire pounded the Japanese to keep them pinned down to their positions.

When the dawn came, lazy and leaden, the foothold was still there, and already beginning to inch forward into the debris of shell holes and splintered coconut trees. The naval bombardment—though it had not had the promised effect—had at least damaged the enemy communications so severely that the Japanese had not been able to organize a counterattack. The crucial hours of the battle were over.

The wade to the beach went on. In some places at first it was as horrible as the preceding day. Gradually, however, as the push inland progressed, the enemy fire across the reef began to diminish. Reserve troops were thrown in, and by afternoon the fight had become a slugging melee for one pillbox after another.

For forty-eight hours the marines fought their way across the island. The Japanese resisted furiously. On the night of the third day they made a last convulsive try. They charged in a mass, yelling their warcry, "Banzai!" One rifle company took the brunt of the assault. The marines knifed, bayoneted, grenaded and clubbed. Again and again, fighting on sheer nerve, they belted the Japanese back.

That ended the heavy fighting. At 1:12 P.M., November 23rd, the Division commander, General Julian Smith, announced that Betio was in marine hands. In four days 984 marines had been killed and 2,072 wounded. Only seventeen Japanese surrendered; the rest were dead. Special units came ashore to garrison Betio and to clean up the carnage. So the

2nd Marine Division returned to its ships, columns of young faces suddenly grown old.

Iwo Jima

Lieutenant General Tadamichi Kuribayashi of the Japanese Army was a short brown man with a plump belly which, it was reported in Tokyo, was "full of fine fighting spirit." He was also one of the most skillful soldiers the marines confronted in their Pacific campaigns. He commanded the 23,000 defenders of Iwo Jima, an island only 660 miles from Tokyo. He knew, as the marines themselves knew, that the time would come when Iwo Jima would have to be assaulted. With its fine airfields, it stood like a barricade in the path of the American offensive.

General Kuribayashi fortified the island's eight square miles with all the patience and skill at his command. At one end of it stood an extinct volcano, Mount Suribachi. In it, the Japanese burrowed like moles, digging caves in which they mounted guns of many calibers.

From the foot of Suribachi the land rose to the north in a series of flat terraces, where the airfields were located, and then humped into crags, gullies and jagged rock. Defending every inch of Iwo Jima, Kuribayashi's men built concrete pillboxes set deep in the soil so that they were scarcely visible. They were connected by underground tunnels that opened up here and there into big rooms where the Japanese commanders controlled the defense network. Artillery pieces, huge mortars, rocket launchers, coastal cannon, and thousands of machine guns were emplaced so that they could hurl metal at every square foot of land. Then General Kuribayashi and his troops waited in their labyrinth for the marines.

The attack began on February 19, 1945. Three Marine Divisions participated—the 3rd, 4th and 5th, totaling more than 60,000 men, all under the command of Major General Harry Schmidt. It was the biggest amphibious operation the marines had ever attempted and into it went the experience of three years of landings in the Pacific. Weeks before it began, American planes bombed Kuribayashi's stronghold. Three days before, a fleet of battleships, cruisers and destroyers began shelling it and continued until H-hour.

Square-jawed barges crept through the haze that morning. They were called LSTs (Landing Ship Tanks), and they formed in a line thousands of yards from the beach. Giant doors in their bows swung apart, and "alligators" swarmed out of their bellies loaded with the assault troops. Kicking up spouts of foam as their tracks churned through the water, the "alligators" seemed to scurry about aimlessly like hordes of water bugs. Soon, however, they were circling in many little groups. One by one they peeled off into lines and as the warships heightened their fire, they began the fateful run to the beach.

Strangely, the island was quiet. Only a few scattered shots greeted the assaulting battalions. Would this be an easy one—at last—for the marines?

For an hour the wily Japanese general waited. He saw with satisfaction that the marines were having trouble on the beach which was not sand but soft, volcanic ash. The "alligators" barely lurched across it, and some of them bogged down hopelessly. The troops found themselves sinking up to their calves in the muck which clung like quicksand. The forward rush of the assault slowed to a painful plod. Succeeding waves piled up behind it so that the beach, as General Kuribayashi had hoped, became a wallowing congestion of men and equipment. He gave the order to fire.

The entire face of Suribachi and every scowling crag and knoll in sight poured forth shot and shells.

From the north, too, came the muffled gun blasts of mortars and artillery hurling barrage after barrage. The effect was appalling.

The plan nearly worked and for several hours that day, no more marines could be landed into the inferno. But General Kuribayashi had made two errors in his planning. He did not realize that the marines had learned to put ashore many troops with lots of equipment in remarkably short periods of time. In that first hour of grace, they landed virtually everything they needed to carry on an attack—tanks, artillery and even bulldozers to cut roads through the ash. The Japanese general also underestimated the determination of his enemy.

Who were these marines who kept pushing through Kuribayashi's barrages? They were young men—many not over nineteen years old—and they came from all parts of America. Most of them were not fighters by profession, but were reservists who joined when the war came and expected to quit when the war was over. Professionals or reservists, they were all marines. They had volunteered in the Corps for one main reason: "to be in a good outfit." They had gone to "Boot Camp" for their first training in the Corps.

"Boot Camp" was a grueling experience. From the first moment, the instructors—hardened noncommissioned officers — were deliberately rough. The "Boots" stood at attention for hours; they were tongue-lashed; they scrubbed the decks with their knuckles; they marched for miles at double-time in sweltering heat; they spent days learning to shoot well, to wriggle under barbed wire and to execute an assault.

At first the "Boots" were dazed or resentful or angry at the treatment. But they grew tough. And when they left "Boot Camp" they were proud of themselves and proud to be marines, convinced that they were tougher than soldiers, sailors or the Japanese. Then, after joining the front line companies in training for combat, their spirit grew deeper. They sensed and learned the unspoken code of loyalty in battle; that marines do not let each other down. They do not bring disgrace on the United States Marine Corps, whose proudest tradition is to accomplish any mission given it no matter how high the odds against it.

An example of this spirit is the story of Sergeant Basilone, one of the marines slogging across the beach at Iwo Jima. At Guadalcanal he had fought off a Japanese attack alone, charging with a machine gun held in his arms until he sank to the ground with wounds. Back in America he was a national hero. Yet he became bored with the tame life in the barracks. The only reward he really wanted for his heroism was the chance to fight again. He even refused an officer's commission. So he had his way and was sent back to the Pacific.

After landing at Iwo Jima, Basilone had to get his guns inland where they could be of use. He led his platoon through the fragments and the volcanic muck toward the first ground rise. There John Basilone met his end, simply because he wanted to be a fighting marine once again. His last words to the men who crouched over him as he died were: "Come on, you guys, we gotta get these guns off the beach———"

Gradually the assaulting battalions were able to bring their tanks and guns to bear and punch out from the beach. In the late afternoon, the reserve battalions stormed ashore. They left a trail of dead and wounded, but they got through to give the attack the momentum it needed. By dusk, Iwo Jima had been cut in two.

The next day one regiment began the assault of Mount Suribachi, known among the marines as the

"Hot Rock." Clearing out the Japanese caves on the Hot Rock was slow and costly. The marines, advancing 200 yards a day, lost 1000 men on the face of the mountain.

On the fourth day at 10:35 A.M. a forty-man patrol gained the summit. They had brought with them a small American flag which they proudly raised on a piece of Japanese pipe. Three hours later a larger flag was hoisted over Suribachi, one that could be seen all over the island and from the ships lying off shore. As this flag was raised, a press photographer named Joe Rosenthal took a picture of the scene. The photograph became famous. Paintings, statues and even a United States stamp were copied from it, as it became a symbol of Marine gallantry in the Pacific.

Meanwhile, the rest of the three divisions were butting northward into General Kuribayashi's main line of defense. It held like rock. But as each assault failed, the determination of the marines to crack it stiffened.

On the fifth day, the unexpected happened. One battalion on the line jumped off in an attack. It was stopped in its tracks. Another battalion assaulted through it and—miraculously—kept going, driving a wedge into the enemy's line. Immediately, every available tank and marine were rushed into the wedge which broadened and surged deeper. In ninety minutes the marines won a parcel of torn land 1000 yards wide and 200 yards deep. On it they counted 800 Japanese pillboxes and block-houses.

The break-through was the beginning of a long and bitter end. Day after day, the marines inched to the north. Their casualties were fearful as entire companies were ground to nothing. Replacements were hurried in to fill the ranks, but these too were whittled away. Frequently the marines overran the pillboxes without knowing they were there. Thus, they would be struck by murderous fire from behind. One captain was directing his company from a hump of ground which he thought was a natural knoll. Suddenly the knoll shook with a muffled explosion. The captain was lying on top of a Japanese block-house housing a big gun which had just opened fire on the beach.

General Kuribayashi began to see that the end was in sight. He sent a radio message to his superiors in Tokyo. He desperately needed ships, planes and troops. The Japanese Navy, most of which was now at the bottom of the ocean, could do nothing. The Japanese airforce tried to help him, but their planes could not break through the ring of air cover the United States Navy had thrown up around Iwo Jima. So Kuribayashi and his troops settled down to kill as many more marines as they could before they themselves would die. In vain the marine command tried to persuade the General by radio to surrender. The General's only answer was a grim silence. So the senseless killing went on.

By March 25th, the Japanese were cornered in a tiny pocket of rock and caves. That night they broke out of it in a counterattack which rampaged across an airfield. Confusion reigned in the darkness, but in the light of day, the last of the defenders were killed. Somewhere in the rubble of Iwo Jima—but never found—lay the rotund body of Kuribayashi.

Thus ended the bloodiest campaign in Marine Corps history. Dead: 5,324; wounded: 16,090.

Korea: 1950, Continued
11

THE MARINES came back from the Pacific with
their prestige higher than at any other time in their
history. They had fought and won one of the most
crucial phases of the war. They had seen their own
amphibious doctrines, which they had spent years
developing, adopted by the Army and by America's
Allies in the Pacific, in Africa and in Europe.

The marines came home also to a climate of peace
and a feeling of thankful relief that the war was

over. It did not seem possible to most of the American people, nor the government that represented them, that armed strength would be needed again soon. Reservists of all the services went home. The military budgets were trimmed bare, and the Marine Corps found itself reduced from 485,000 men to some 77,000—10,000 less than the casualties it suffered in World War II.

Then, on June 25, 1950, the country was shocked by news from a far-off part of the world. The North Korean Communist Army, spearheaded by Russian-made tanks, had rumbled across the 38th Parallel into the Republic of South Korea.

This time America fought under the banner of the United Nations. The South Korean Army was no match for the Russian-trained North Koreans. From Japan, General Douglas MacArthur, Commander in Chief of the United Nations Forces, rushed American soldiers into South Korea. They delayed the Red columns while other Army divisions flung up a defense around Pusan, a vital South Korean port. Soon the North Koreans were striking at the Pusan perimeter. The outnumbered Army divisions and the South Koreans held desperately to their precarious foothold and waited for reinforcements.

The marines had been to Korea before in 1871.

On August 2, 1950, they returned. A brigade under Brigadier General Edward Craig joined the hard-pressed army from Pusan. Lieutenant General Walton Walker, MacArthur's field commander, used the marines as a fire brigade. He moved them from place to place along the perimeter, throwing them into the danger zones to snuff out North Korean attacks. The brigade fought across rice fields and blistering hot ridges.

A war correspondent, James Bell, described a marine assault on a nameless piece of land defended by 600 North Koreans. "As the assault force came down into the valley, they were met with a hail of fire . . . they moved across the valley and up the barren face of the ridge. Everywhere along the assault line men dropped. This appeared to be impossible but, all glory forever to the bravest men I ever saw, the line did not break. It went forward in short spurts. The casualties were unthinkable, but the assault force never turned back. It moved, fell down, got up and moved again.

"For more than an hour, the assault force stumbled and struggled forward . . . Then with a final thrust, an estimated ten marines reached the northern crest. They never came back.

"It is nice to report," went on James Bell, "that the second assault wave carried the ridge with no name and that the marines continued to advance, taking their objectives as they came . . ."

In September the brigade was pulled off the Pusan perimeter to join two marine regiments freshly arrived from America. Thus, the First Marine Division was reformed, and placed under the command of Major General O. P. Smith.

The Division played a big role in General Mac-Arthur's defeat of the North Koreans. It made a landing deep in enemy territory on the west coast of the Korean peninsula. Striking inland, it captured the city of Seoul, hub of the enemy supply lines. At the same time, the Army broke out of the Pusan perimeter. Thousands of North Koreans were killed and captured. To complete the victory, MacArthur sent his divisions across the 38th parallel.

The marines boarded ships again and were taken to the east coast of the peninsula where they made a landing at the North Korean port of Wonsan. They marched up the coast to another city, Hung-nam, where a great plain stretched out before them. Beyond it, mountains rose high in the distant mist.

The marines were ordered to march into these

mountains to trap remnants of the North Korean army. But disturbing news, meanwhile, had spread across the war front. The Chinese Communists were threatening to enter the war. Already, in fact, "volunteer" units of Chinese were said to have come down from the north into the mountains of North Korea. Behind them some 300,000 Chinese soldiers were known to be massed on the boundary, possibly to be thrown into the war.

Would it be wise to advance into the mountains where units could be ambushed and trapped by the Chinese hordes? The question was weighed. Mac-Arthur, gambling that the Chinese would stay out, said to advance. His lieutenants repeated the order. The marines and soldiers obeyed.

The First Marine Division set out across the plain toward the mountains. It plodded into the foothills where the regiments split off into different valleys that wound northward. It was late autumn now. The weather was brisk, and as the days and miles went by, it grew colder. The hills merged into mountains that rose, forbiddingly steep, ahead.

If the Chinese had not officially entered the war, they were certainly fighting it. At first there were skirmishes. Then battles.

Still the order remained: advance. At Sudong—

a cluster of brown shacks on the valley road—the 7th Regiment fought and killed hundreds of Chinese. The enemy charged down a valley at night, but the marine artillery, ricocheting its shells along the rocky slopes, cut them to pieces.

It was at Sudong, too, that the 2nd platoon of Company E, commanded by Lieutenant John Yancey, assaulted Hill 698. Only a handful of men were left in the 2nd platoon, but replacements soon brought it up to strength.

Trudging up the valley mile after mile, Yancey felt hemmed in by time and space. The cold had become intense. Rations and drinking water froze solid. Men suffered from frostbite. Every evening, when the long column stopped, foxholes had to be hacked out of the frozen earth as a precaution against the Chinese attacks which came screaming out of the ridges. When Yancey asked the civilians in the villages how many Chinese they had seen, the answer was always the same: "Many, many Chinese— maybe 40,000."

The 7th Regiment came to a village called Yudam-ni which lay near the bank of a reservoir. Company E filed along the road, jammed with trucks, jeeps, tanks, and guns, to the bottom of a long narrow ridge that faced to the north. On Yancey's map, it was Hill 1282. Its surface was hidden by six inches of snow through which protruded occasional clumps of forlorn twigs. Slowly the men climbed to the ridge, sagging under the sixty to seventy pounds of equipment they carried. With Chinese picks and shovels which they had found in a village, they dug in along the crest of 1282, as they always did at night.

Yancey's platoon defended the north side of the ridge facing a looming mass of high ground which, to Yancey, seemed particularly ominous. From it, saddles of land fingered toward his position—fine routes of approach for attacking Chinese. One of them came directly into Hill 1282. At this point, he placed a machine gun. The gunner was Gallagher, the powerful black-haired marine who had braved the Chinese fire at Hill 698 to save the 2nd platoon. Out in front of Gallagher, Yancey placed a trip flare that could be lighted if an attack came. He scattered the rest of his men along the ridges so that the other approaches were covered.

All was quiet that night except for a brief interlude which convinced Yancey that an attack would be made. A Chinese platoon probed the line at various places to discover the locations of his guns. Among the dead was a Chinese officer with mapmaking equipment and a tape measure to plot the exact marine positions. During the following day, patrols engaged swarms of Chinese in the hills facing Company E's position.

A ghostly fog crept up the valley at dusk, hiding the top of the mountains. Yancey sat near his foxhole. With his bayonet he dug a hole in the ground, laid some twigs in it and lit a fire to heat his can of meat and beans. After he had eaten, he crawled into his sleeping bag, which he placed in his foxhole.

In less than an hour, he was out of the foxhole again. Small groups of Chinese began harassing the company line, probing again to locate gun positions. At first the attacks were sporadic. But gradually they seemed to grow stronger, and Yancey guessed that the Chinese were building up for an assault.

Then, in front of Gallagher's position, came the sounds of many feet crunching in the snow. Gallagher waited until the crunching was loud and he could see shadows flickering in the half-light of the moon. At that moment he pulled the trip flare which revealed a mass of Chinese. Seconds later he pulled the trigger. The Chinese blew their bugles, horns and whistles, and charged.

Yancey, jumping to his phone, was shouting orders to the mortar crews: "Lay in on the ridge and work back!" The shells pummeled the finger of land

and the entire line of Yancey's platoon raked it with bullets. After ten minutes Gallagher could stop firing. A foot in front of him lay the last soldier of the first Chinese assault.

For fifteen minutes there was a lull in the battle. Then mortar shells thundered on top of Company E. Deadly accurate, they smashed into the marine foxholes, burning and killing relentlessly. And even as the shelling went on the Chinese threw themselves against the marine line. On they came, bugles blowing, cursing at the marines in English. Three waves of them were mowed down.

Yancey darted up and down the line, shouting to his men to fix bayonets. A fragment of metal slashed through his nose. For a moment he could not breathe, but he spat out the blood that clogged his throat and went about his business. Crouching low, he ran from one gun position to another. To his surprise he saw Robinson, the private who weeks ago had taken command of a squad and had led it up the face of Hill 698. Miles back down the valley road, Yancey had left Robinson in the field hospital with frozen feet; but upon hearing that Company E was in trouble, Robinson had forced his way from the hospital tent and, hobbling painfully, had come to help out in the middle of the battle.

Until 5 A.M. the Chinese assaulted every fifteen or twenty minutes. Not once did they penetrate the marine line. But their ammunition had run low; there were only six mortar shells left; phone lines were shattered; how many marines were left alive was not known then; and there were many wounded.

The Chinese shifted their tactics. They came in on the flank of Company E. Tossing volleys of grenades and firing their "burp" guns from their hips, they overran a machine-gun position. More Chinese poured into the opening, spreading out into the Company mortar emplacements. They were on the ridge now. Unless a line was formed to check the breakthrough, 1282 would be lost.

The commander of Company E, Captain Walter Phillips, formed the line. He seized a rifle with a bayonet fixed to it and drove it into the ground. "Nobody goes behind this point!" he bellowed. He was shot, and fell dead at the foot of the rifle. Nobody fell back behind it. Lieutenant Ball, sitting as he fired, was hit many times before he shot his last bullet.

Yancey, meanwhile, was leading a counterattack against the Chinese who were dodging up over the ridge. As he turned to shout to the men he led, he saw that they had all been shot. He was alone. The Chinese were running toward him. At that instant a grenade burst in front of him. A fragment buried itself in the roof of his mouth. The explosion blew him over backwards down a slope. As he rolled over and over, exploding grenades followed him but miraculously he was not hit again.

The Chinese were pressing on toward the line Captain Phillips had drawn. The moment of the battle had been reached where the slightest pressure either way would turn the tide. As he lay in the snow, Yancey could hardly breathe; between breaths he coughed blood. But in the savage pitch of the fight he barely noticed his wounds. He stood up. At this moment he heard himself shouting the famous battle cry used on Guadalcanal by the Marine Raiders: "Gung Ho!" Someone else heard it above the din and yelled it too. It was picked up here, then there, and finally went surging through the men of Company E who could still walk. Most were already wounded but they formed into a line led by Yancey, a grim, bloody figure as he gripped his rifle. They charged the Chinese, with their bayonets fixed. The burp guns rattled, the grenades blasted, but the marines could not be stopped.

Yancey saw a flash in front of him. A hot, thudding bullet struck him in the right cheek. He fell forward on his knee. He could not see out of one eye now. Out of the other one he saw his men, shadowy in the light of the dawn, finishing off the remnants of the Chinese attack. Painfully, with his hand clenched over his right eye, he walked back to the top of the ridge, where he sank to the snow.

One hundred and eighty-one men had filed up to Hill 1282 three days before. Thirty-six of them filed off it. Around it lay almost 1000 dead Chinese. Lieutenant Yancey was flown out of Yudam-ni in a helicopter. The bullet that had hit him had lodged in the back of his neck. It was removed; he lived and regained the sight of his eye.

Actions like the battle of Hill 1282 occurred many times around the Chosin Reservoir. The Chinese swarmed confidently out of the mountains, but the marines held their perimeters. Then, when the orders finally came to withdraw, they marched down the valley and cut through any enemy force which chose to block their way.

They emerged onto the plain, and when they reached Hungnam, the ships were waiting in the harbor to take them to a rest area. There the gaps in their ranks would be filled and marines would be ready again for the next campaign, wherever it might be.

Index

LANDMARK BOOKS

★